AF618261

creamy feelings curdle

Ellen Akimoto

KERBER ART

Selbstbewusste Malerei

Im Jahr 2017 malte Ellen Akimoto ein Bild, dem sie den Titel „The Lower Left Hand Corner of Such a Good Painting" gab. Es unterscheidet sich von vielen anderen ihrer Bilder, da es aus nur drei Elementen besteht: einem Parkettfußboden, einer weißen Wand, einem an ihr hängenden abstrakten Gemälde. Perspektive und Bildausschnitt sind so gewählt, dass die drei Sujets jeweils nur zum Teil zu sehen sind. So entsteht zwar ein illusionistischer Bildraum, doch fällt es nicht schwer, das Bild genauso als Abfolge von drei Flächen zu betrachten. Akimotos Bild hat damit den Charakter eines Kippbildes: Es lässt sich entweder als gegenständliches oder als abstraktes Bild wahrnehmen. Und da es als gegenständliches Bild ein abstraktes Gemälde als Sujet hat, wiederholt sich derselbe Gegensatz von ‚gegenständlich' und ‚abstrakt' nochmals auf anderer Ebene. Durch den Titel wird er sogar ein weiteres Mal zum Thema, weist dieser doch das abstrakte Bild im gegenständlichen Bild als „so ein gutes Gemälde" aus. Damit würdigt die gegenständliche Malerin die abstrakte Malerei.

Eine solche Geste wäre jahrzehntelang unvorstellbar gewesen. Während der gesamten Klassischen Moderne gab es klare und strenge Trennlinien – schon zwischen einzelnen Avantgarden und Richtungen, aber erst recht zwischen dem Gebiet gegenständlicher Malerei und dem Bereich abstrakter Kunst. Es waren unterschiedliche, unvereinbare Weltanschauungen, die darin jeweils zur Geltung kamen, und der Kalte Krieg nach 1945 verlieh dem Gegensatz zudem eine stark politische Dimension. Zwar gab es Abweichler, die sich nicht an die Vorgaben hielten und die im Osten abstrakt, im Westen gegenständlich malten, aber statt damit zu einer Entspannung der Fronten zu führen, heizten sie die ideologisch geführten Debatten nur noch weiter an. Mittlerweile ist aber auch das längst so sehr Geschichte wie der Kalte Krieg, und es fällt sogar schon schwer, sich den Richtungsstreit, der einige Generationen von Künstlern in Beschlag nahm, in all seiner Unerbittlichkeit überhaupt noch vorzustellen.

Die heutigen Maler aber profitieren gleich doppelt von dieser Entwicklung. Sie haben nicht nur mehr Möglichkeiten, weil ihnen nun endlich die gesamte Bandbreite an bildnerischen Mitteln und Methoden zur Verfügung steht, sondern ihnen kommt es auch zugute, dass diese in den Jahrzehnten der Trennung jeweils in einer unglaublichen Vielfalt entwickelt worden waren. Gerade weil beide Seiten ihre Überlegenheit und ihre Fortschrittlichkeit beweisen wollten, brachte jeder Ismus und jede Strömung eigene, zusätzliche malerische Möglichkeiten hervor. Im Rückblick erscheint die Moderne wie eine Anzahl von Laboratorien, in denen unter Hochdruck Stil um Stil, Effekt um Effekt, Faktur um Faktur entwickelt wurde. Viele davon wurden dann kaum gebraucht, weil schon die nächsten zur Verfügung standen, andere gingen in Richtungskämpfen unter oder wurden schlicht übersehen. Und sie alle sind nun frei verwendbar, ohne die ideologischen Hypotheken, die auf ihnen ursprünglich lasteten, in nahezu beliebigen Kombinationen und Mischungen.

Ellen Akimotos Malerei liefert viele eindrucksvolle Beispiele dafür, in was für eine reiche Phase ihrer Geschichte die Malerei eingetreten ist. Auf ihren Bildern finden sich Drippings und Striche im Geist des Action Painting direkt neben Partien, die einen Vorhang so plastisch abbilden, dass man die samtige Oberfläche zu spüren glaubt (z.B. „Talking Incomprehensibly About the Leaf", 2019). Oder monochrome Flächen im Stil des Suprematismus tauchen auf demselben Bild auf wie veristisch gemalte Objekte, die an die Malerei der Neuen Sachlichkeit erinnern (z.B. „Nighttime", 2019). Oder ein im Bild gemaltes Landschaftsgemälde verwandelt sich plötzlich in eine abstrakte Malerei, überschreitet den eigenen Rahmen und verschmilzt mit dem Gesicht einer Frau, die auf einem Sofa unter dem Gemälde sitzt („Speaking Persuasively", 2018). Akimoto zitiert also nicht einfach nur Stilmittel aus dem Repertoire der jüngeren Malereigeschichte, sondern stellt sie in überraschende, witzige Beziehungen zueinander und verwandelt sie in ihrer Verbindung in etwas Neues.

Die Gemälde von Ellen Akimoto strahlen daher die Freude unbeschwerten Machens aus. Auf ihnen ist die Malerei voll zu sich gekommen, ja ist im doppelten Sinne selbstbewusst geworden: Indem sie die Stilmittel verschiedener Provenienz gleichermaßen aufgreift und miteinander ins Spiel bringt, reflektiert Akimoto sie zugleich und macht sie sich auf dem jeweiligen Bild selbst bewusst. Damit aber wird auch gegenwärtig, wie viele Möglichkeiten der Malerei zur Verfügung stehen; es wird präsent, was sie stark sein lässt, und daraus bezieht sie Selbstbewusstsein. Dieses Gefühl von Stärke überträgt sich auf die Betrachter. Sie fühlen sich herausgefordert, ihre eigenen Mittel und Möglichkeiten zu erfassen und nicht brachliegen zu lassen. Sie lernen, im Umgang damit ebenfalls unbeschwerter zu werden. Die Freiheit, der sich Akimotos Bilder verdanken, pflanzt sich durch sie also weiter fort.

Wolfgang Ullrich

Self-confident painting

In 2017 Ellen Akimoto painted a picture with the title "The Lower Left Hand Corner of Such a Good Painting". It differs from many of her others in that it consists of only three elements: a parquet floor, a white wall, and, on the wall, an abstract painting. Perspective and framing have been chosen so that only part of each element is visible. An illusionistic pictorial space does emerge from this, but it is also just as easy to envisage the image as a sequence of three surfaces. Akimoto's picture has thereby the character of a reversible figure: it can be seen as either a representational or an abstract image. And because it has, as representational image, an abstract painting as its subject, it repeats the same opposition between "representational" and "abstract" on another level. And through the title the opposition becomes again a theme: the abstract image in the representational image is declared as "such a good painting". With this the representational painter pays tribute to abstract painting.

There were decades in which such a gesture would have been unimaginable. During the period of classical modernism there were clear and strict lines of demarcation — already between individual avant-gardes and trends, but all the more between the field of representational painting and the sphere of abstract art. These were different and irreconcilable outlooks and came into their own as such. The cold war after 1945, moreover, gave the opposition a highly political dimension. Yes, there were dissidents who didn't keep to the guidelines and who painted abstract pictures in the east or representational ones in the west but, instead of this leading to a relaxation of fronts, it fuelled the ideologically-led debates only more. In the meantime, however, all that has passed into history just as much as the cold war, and it is now difficult to even imagine at all the factional disputes, which monopolised some generations of artists, in all their relentlessness.

Today's painters nevertheless profit from this development in two ways. They not only have more possibilities — because the full range of pictorial means and methods are now finally available to them — but they also reap the benefits of these being developed in astonishing variety in the decades of division. Precisely because both sides wanted to prove their superiority and progressiveness, each "ism" and each tendency produced its own additional painterly possibilities. In retrospect the modern period appears as a number of laboratories in which, under high pressure, style upon style, effect upon effect, texture upon texture were developed. Many of these were barely needed then because already the next one was available, others disappeared amongst factional struggles, or were simply overlooked. And now they are all freely usable, in almost any combination and mixture, and without the ideological burdens which were originally laid on them.

Ellen Akimoto's painting offers many impressive examples of what, in that rich phase of its history, emerged into painting. In her pictures one finds drippings and strokes in the manner of action painting directly next to sections that portray a curtain so plastically that one believes one could actually feel the velvety surface (e.g. "Talking Incomprehensibly About the Leaf", 2019). Or monochrome surfaces in the style of Suprematism appear in the same image as apparently strictly naturalistic objects that remind one of the painting of the New Objectivity (e.g. "Nighttime", 2019). Or a landscape painting that is painted into the picture transforms itself suddenly into abstract painting, oversteps its own borders and merges with the face of a woman who sits on a sofa underneath ("Speaking Persuasively", 2018). Akimoto is, then, not merely quoting stylistic devices from the repertoire of the earlier history of painting but also placing them in surprising, witty relationships to each other and transforming them in their connection into something new.

The paintings of Ellen Akimoto radiate the joy of unburdened making. In them painting has fully come to itself, indeed has become confident in a double sense: by taking up stylistic devices of different provenances equally and bringing them into play, Akimoto reflects them and at the same time makes them in each respective picture conscious of themselves. With this it becomes clear how many possibilities there are available in painting; it also becomes clear what makes painting strong, and from this it derives self-confidence. This feeling of strength is transmitted to the viewers. They feel themselves challenged to grasp their own means and possibilities and not to let them lie fallow. They learn in dealing with these to become more carefree. This freedom, which is thanks to Akimoto's pictures, thus continues, through them, to propagate itself.

Wolfgang Ullrich

The Lower Left Hand Corner of Such a Good Painting

Öl und Acryl auf Leinwand, 90×70 cm, 2017

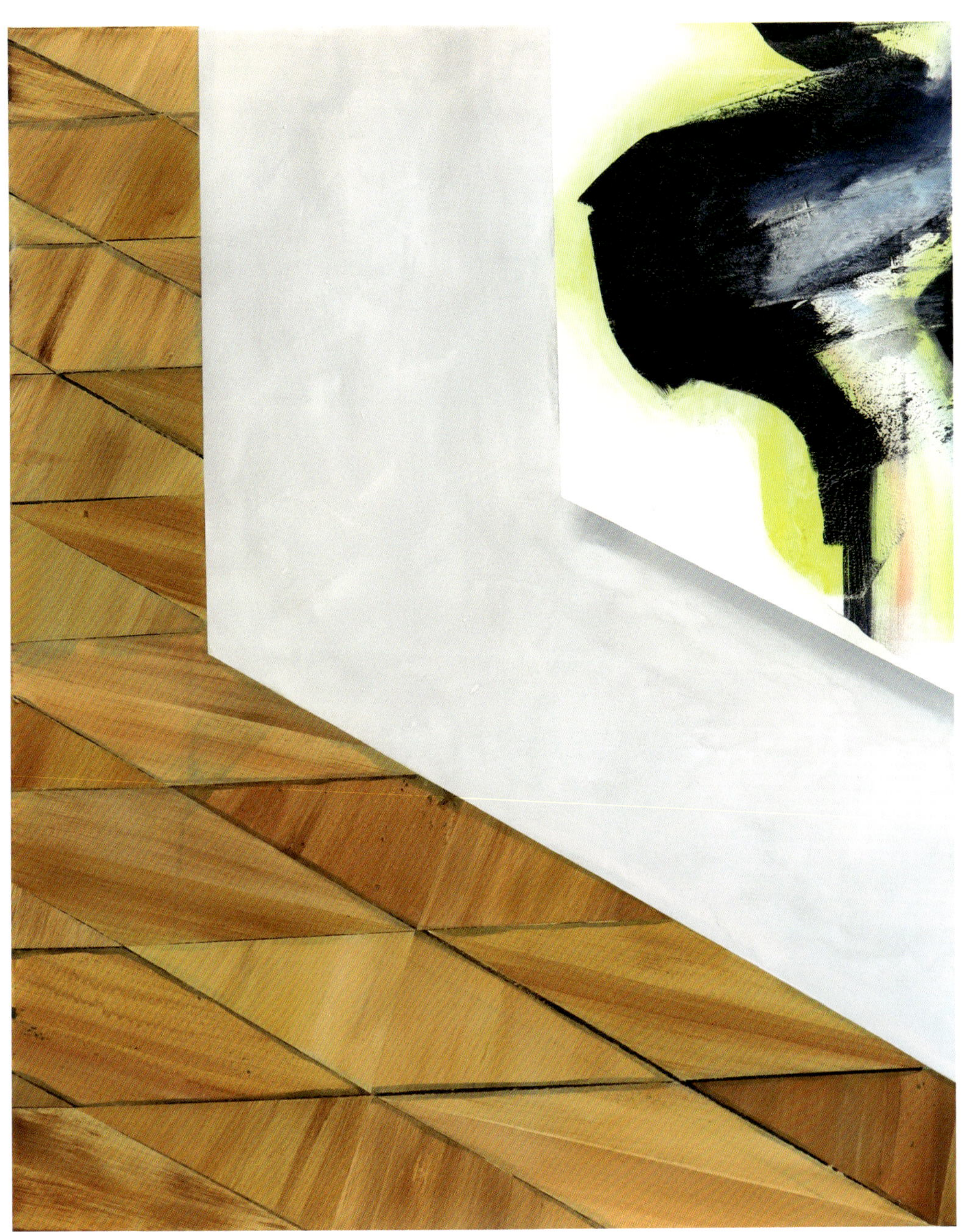

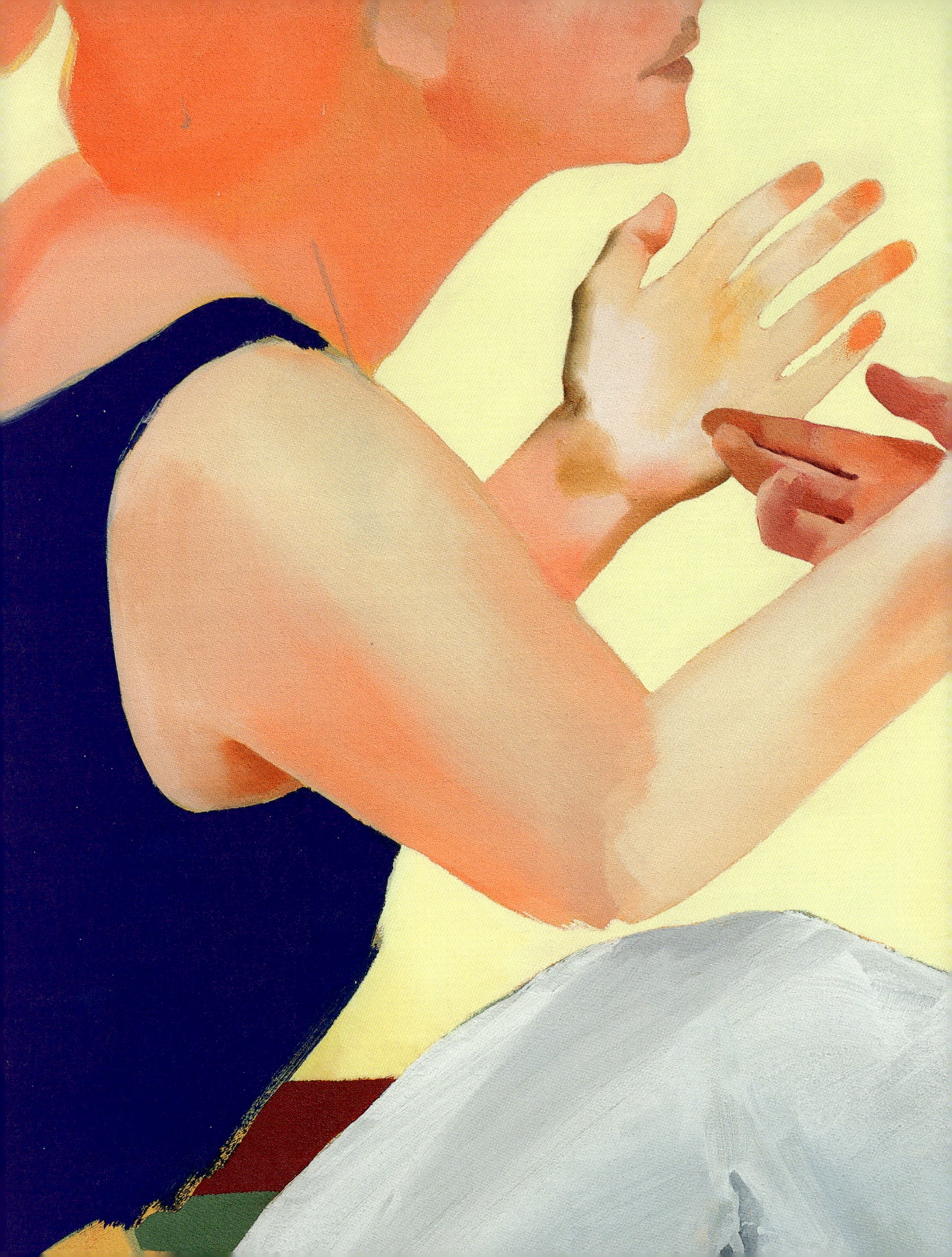

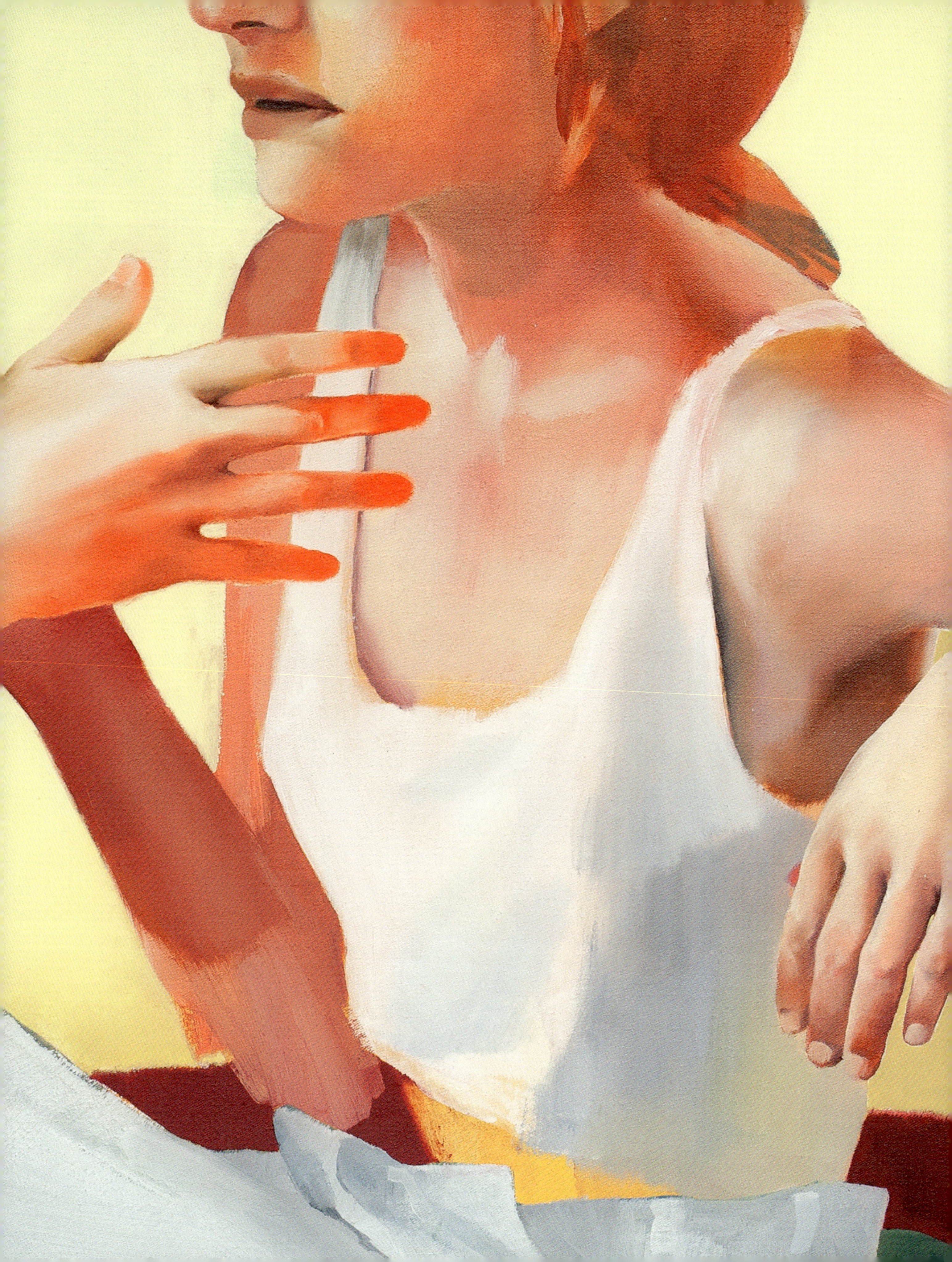

Speaking Intently

Öl und Acryl auf Leinwand, 200 × 150 cm, 2019

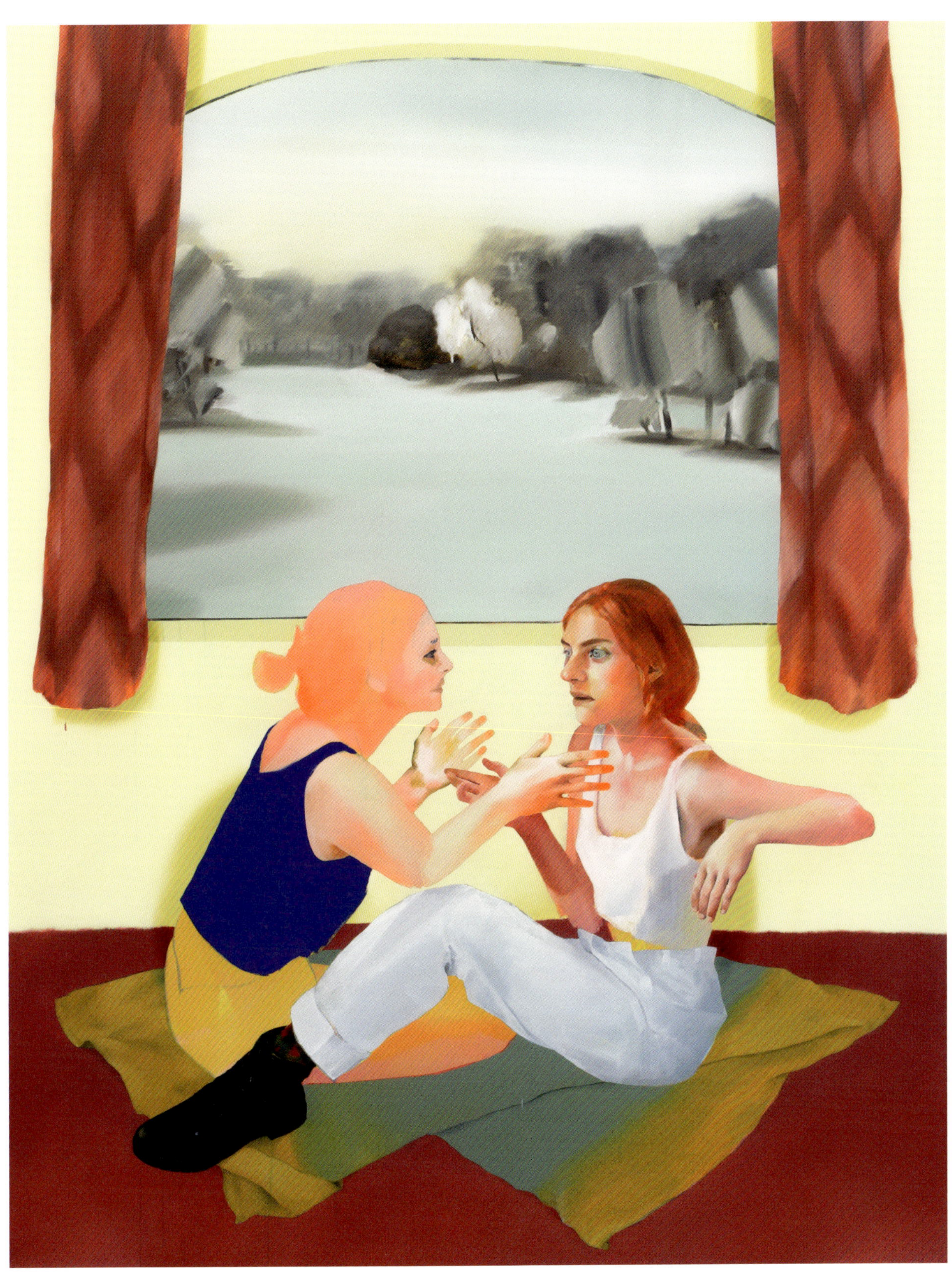

Cat on a Rug

Öl auf Leinwand, 50×60 cm, 2018

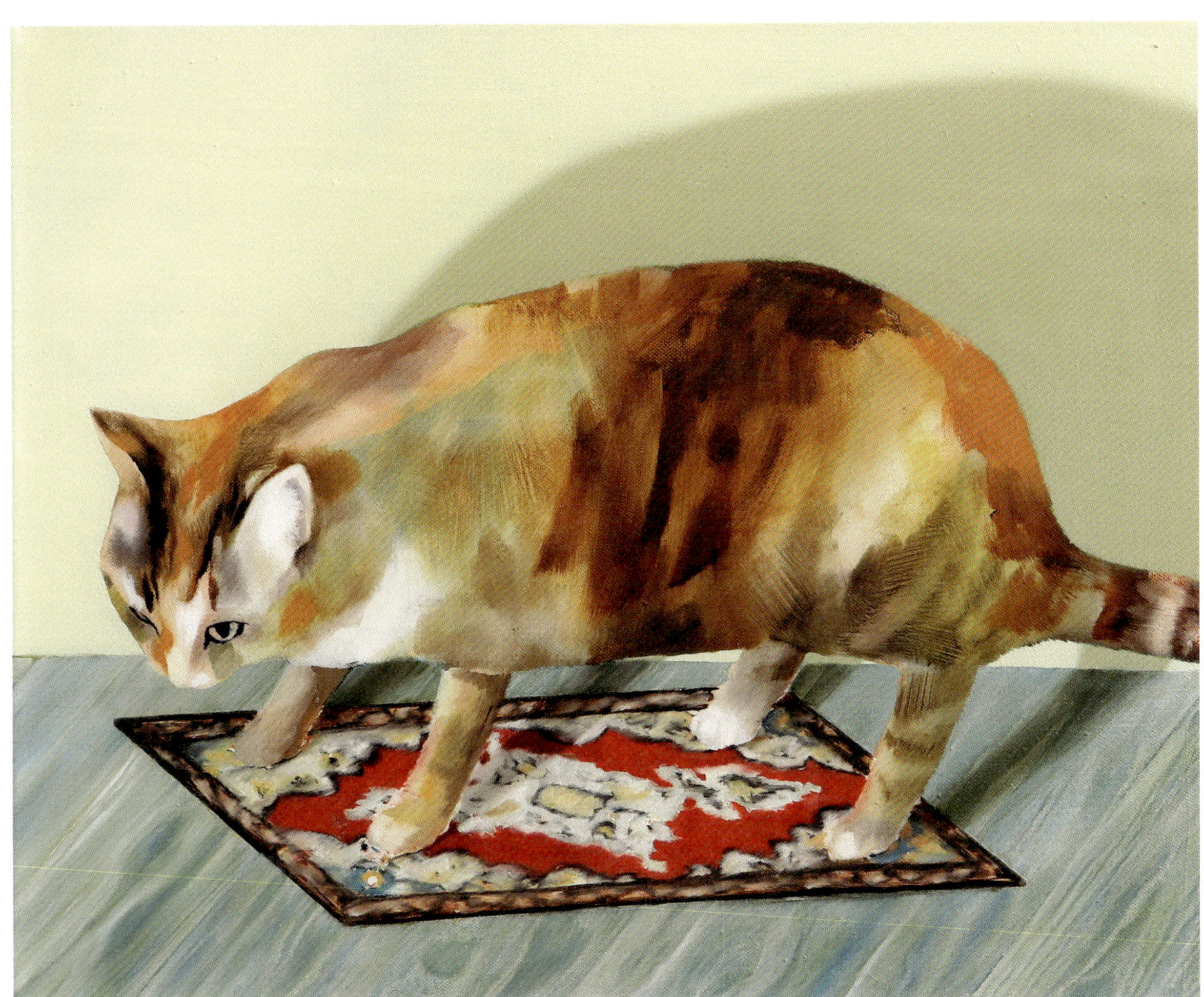

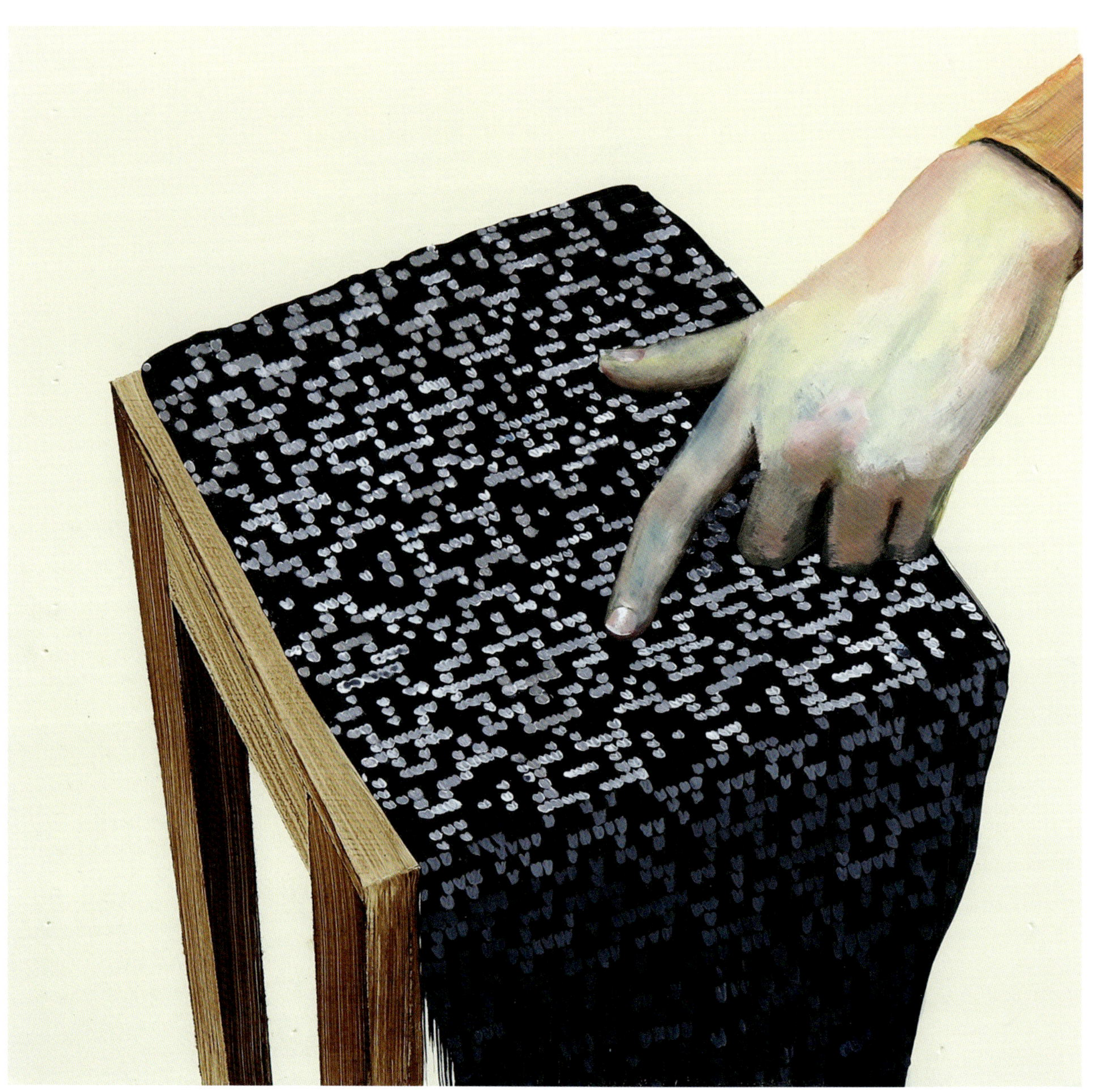

The Point

Acryl auf Holz, 25×25 cm, 2018

On the Cusp

Öl auf Leinwand, 80×60 cm, 2020

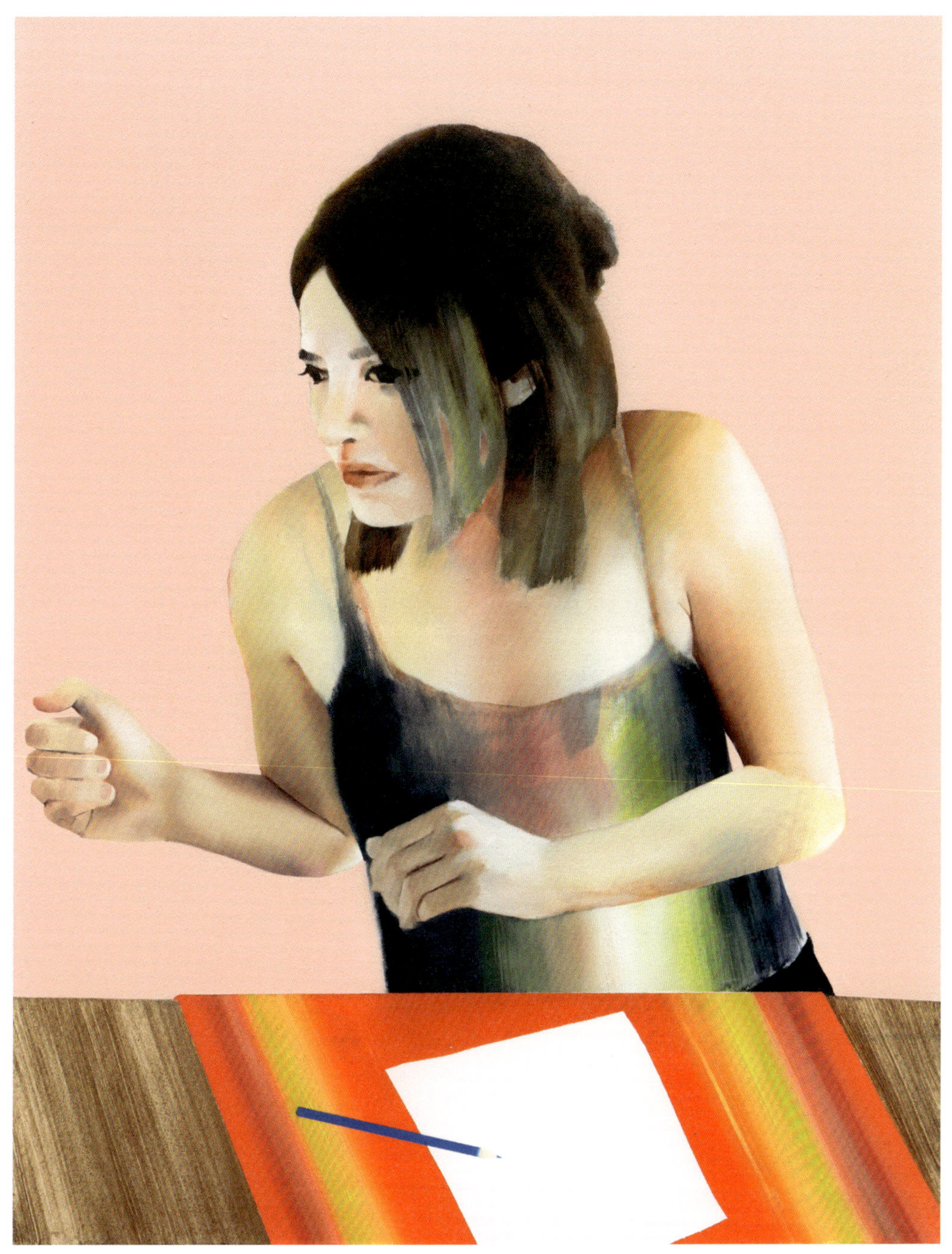

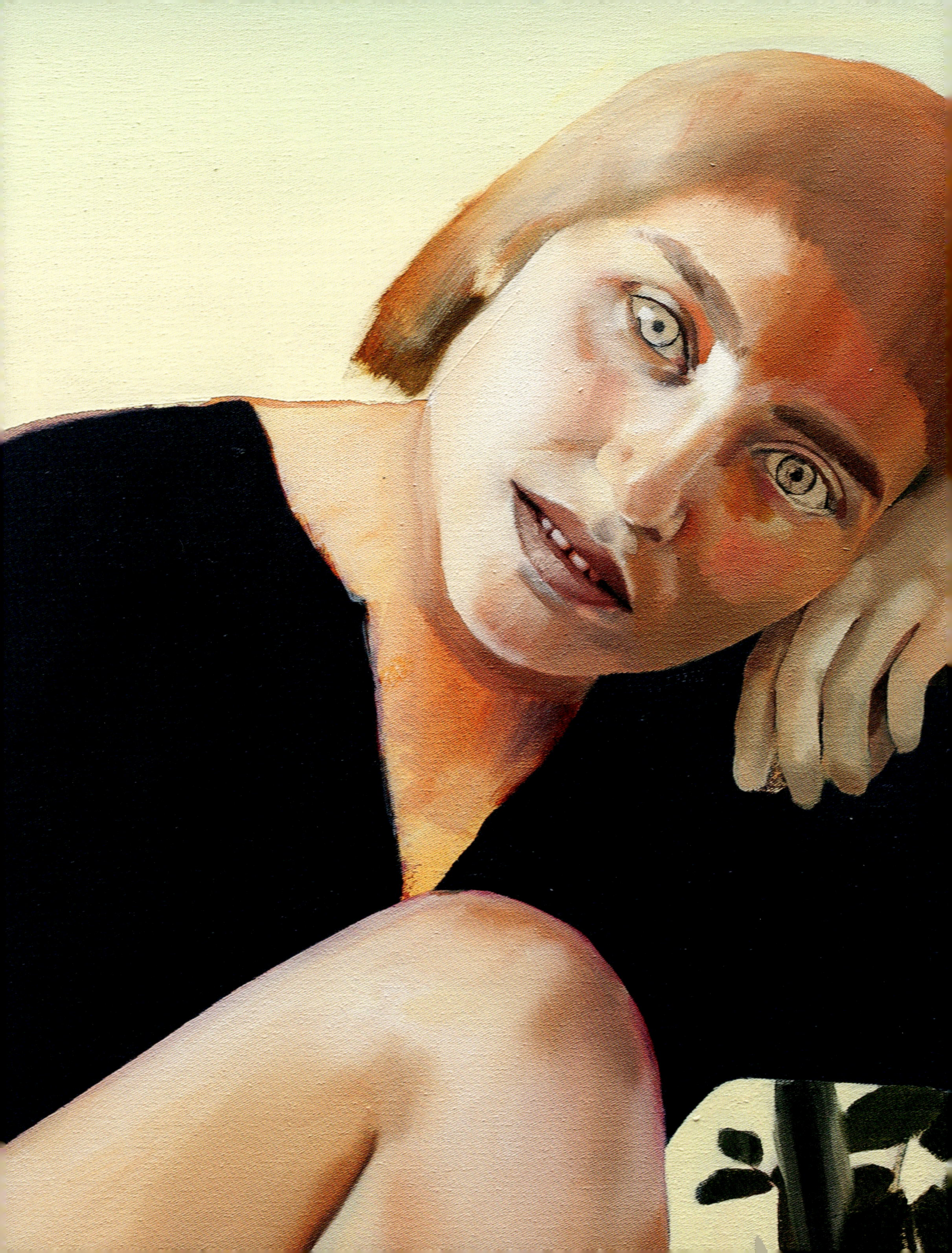

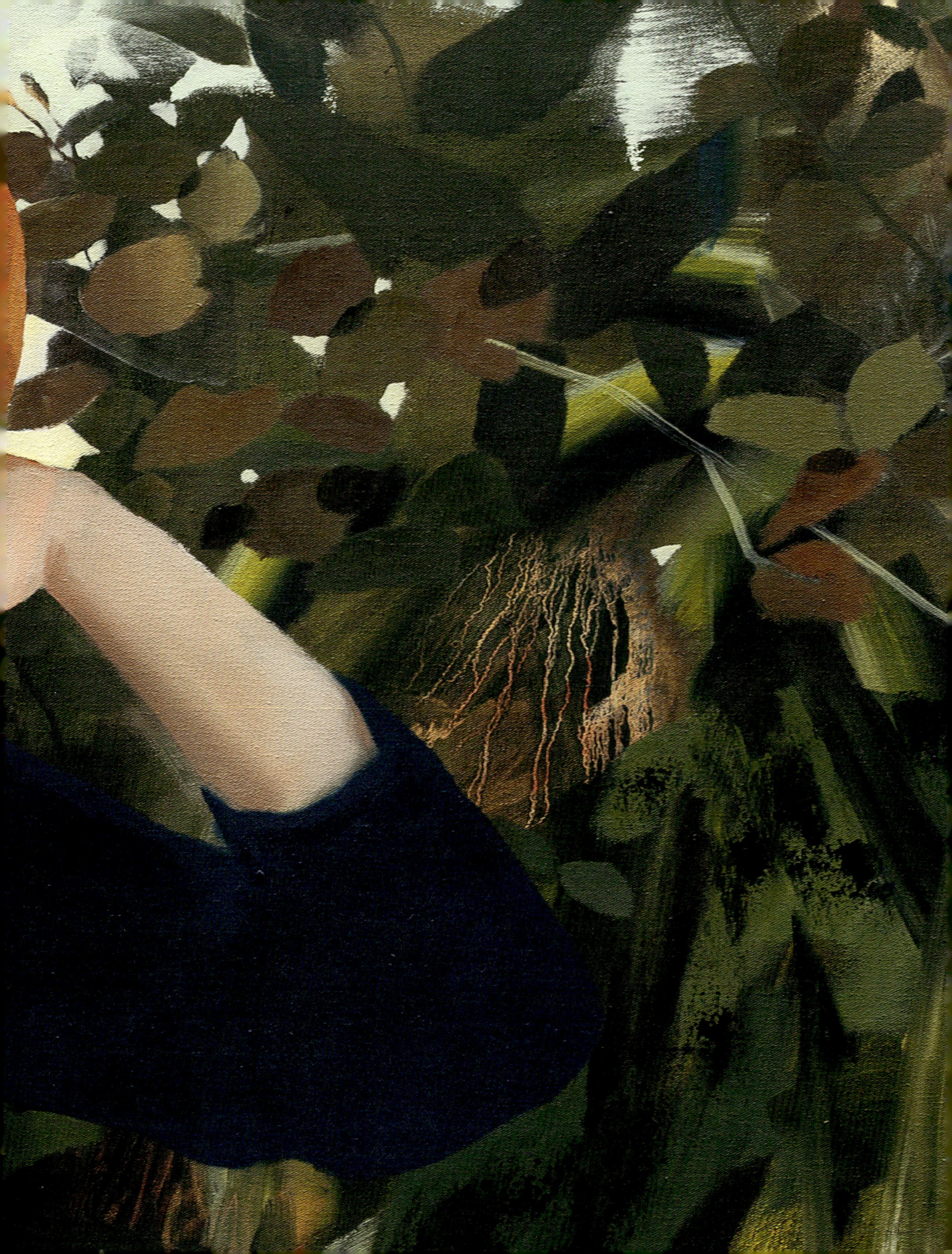

Being Natural

Öl auf Leinwand, 130×110 cm, 2019

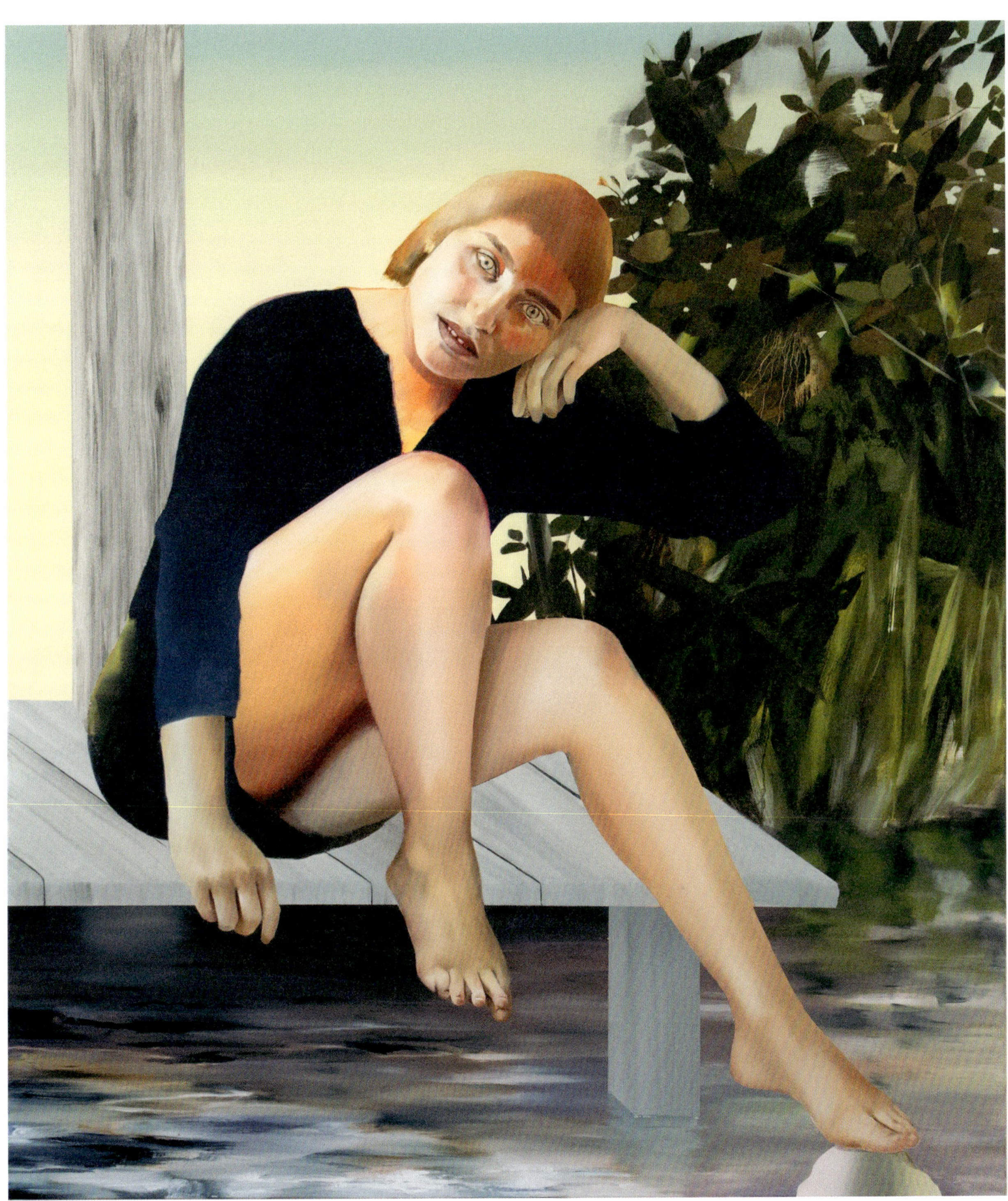

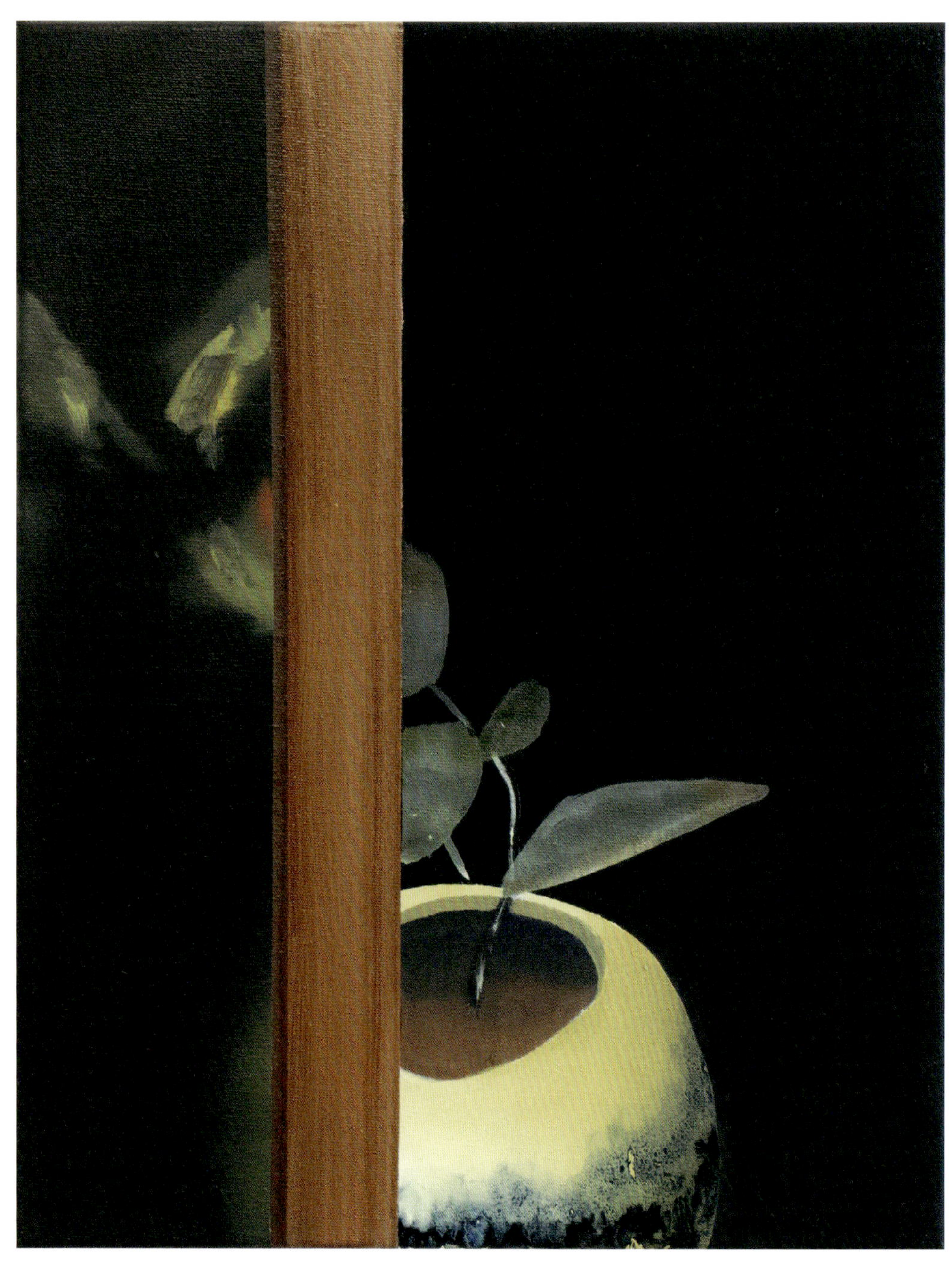

Night Plant

Öl und Acryl auf Leinwand, 40×30 cm, 2019

Holding the Soap

Öl auf Leinwand, 40×30 cm, 2019

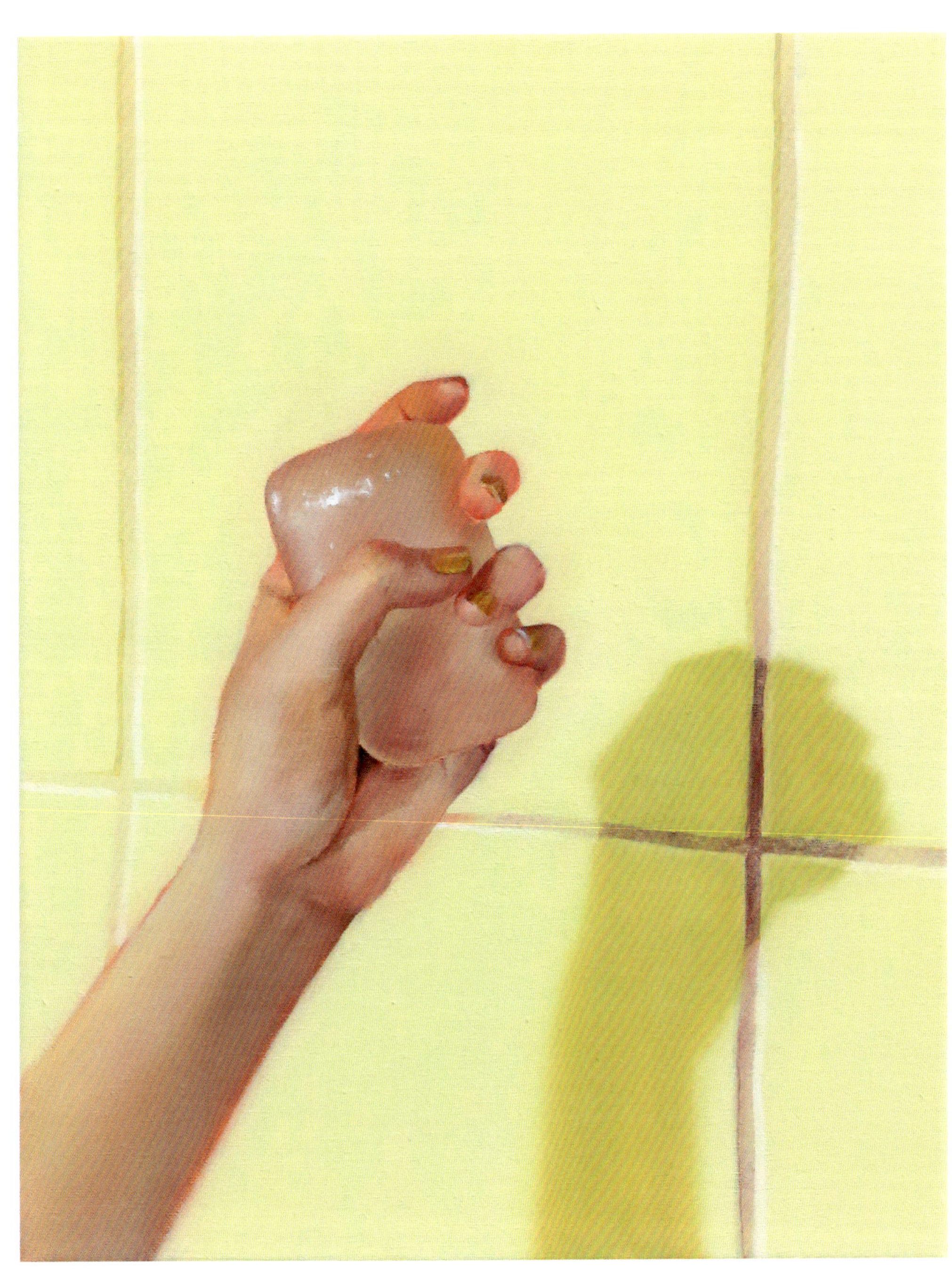

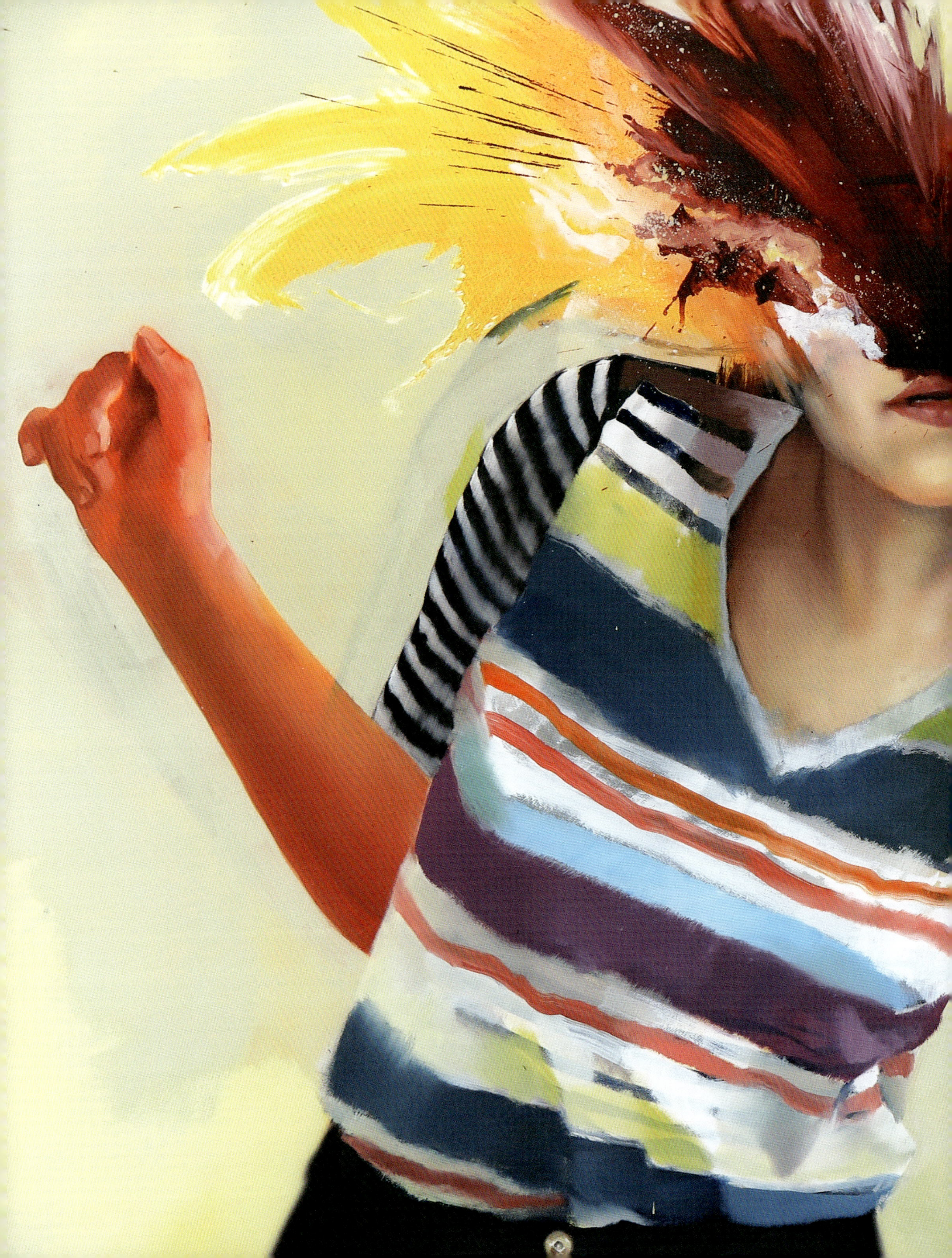

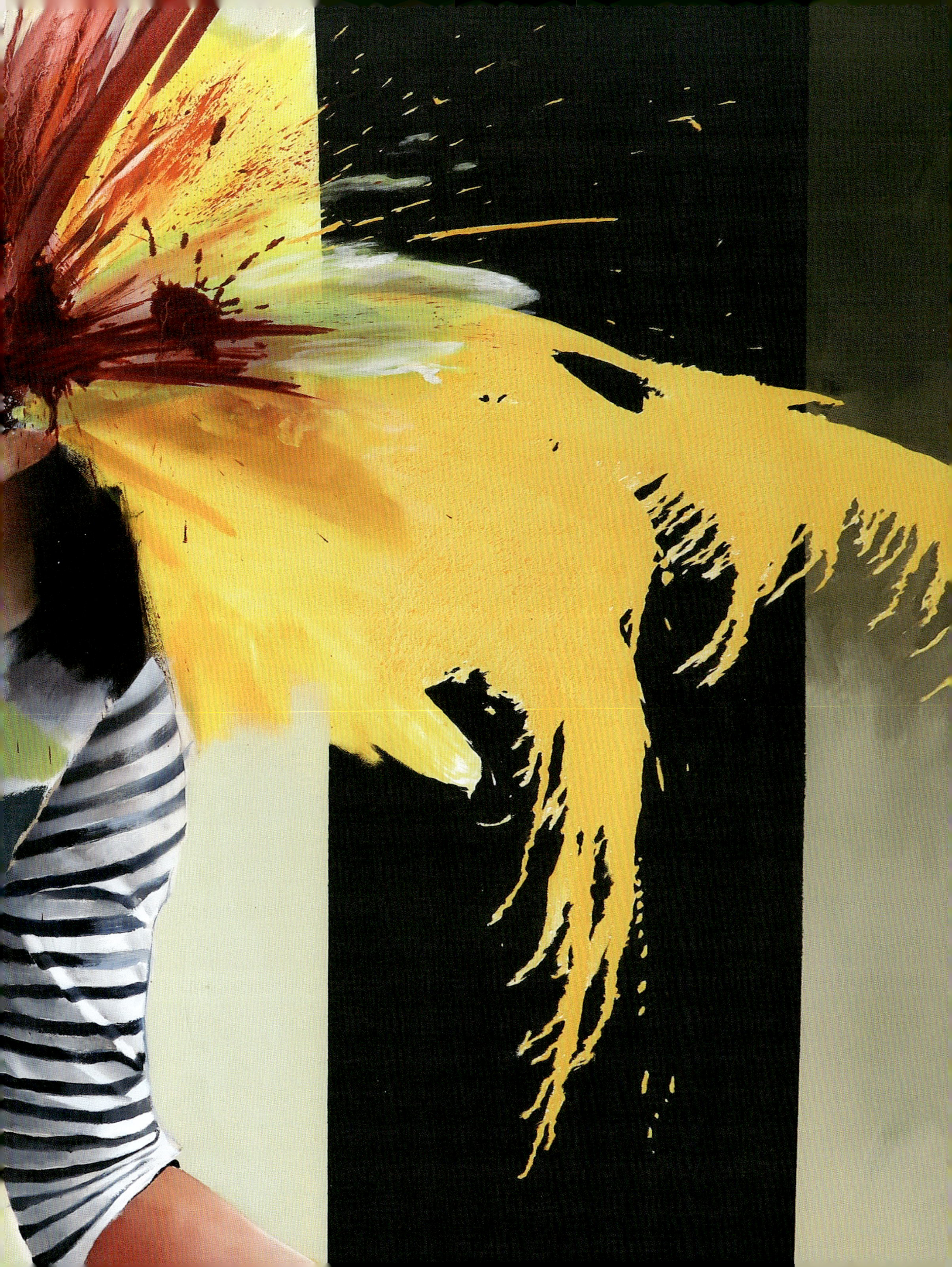

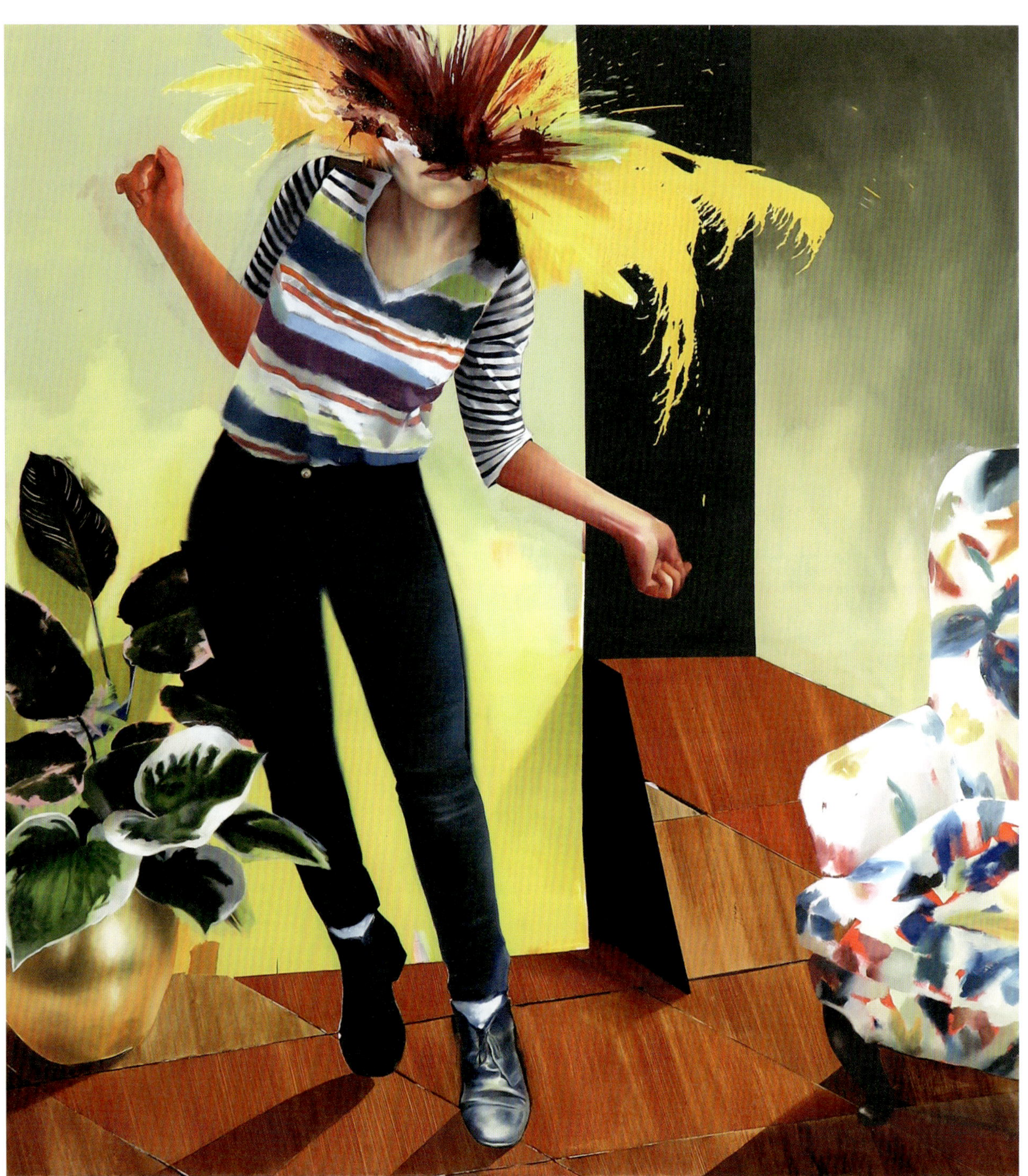

Head Explodes Due to Personal Reasons

Öl auf Leinwand, 160 × 140 cm, 2018

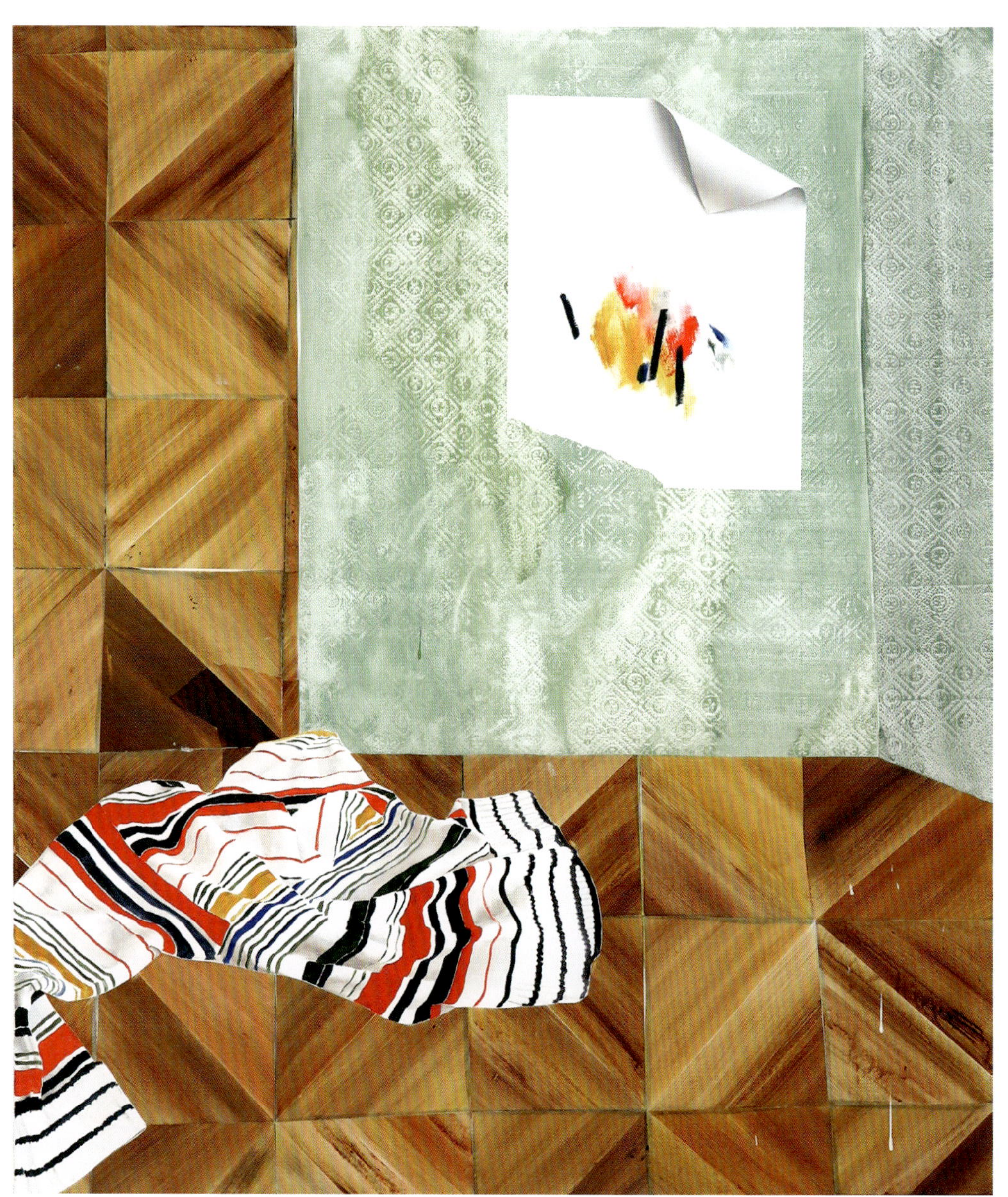

Attempt

Öl und Acryl auf Leinwand, 120 × 100 cm, 2018

Gießkanne

Öl auf Leinwand, 40 × 30 cm, 2019

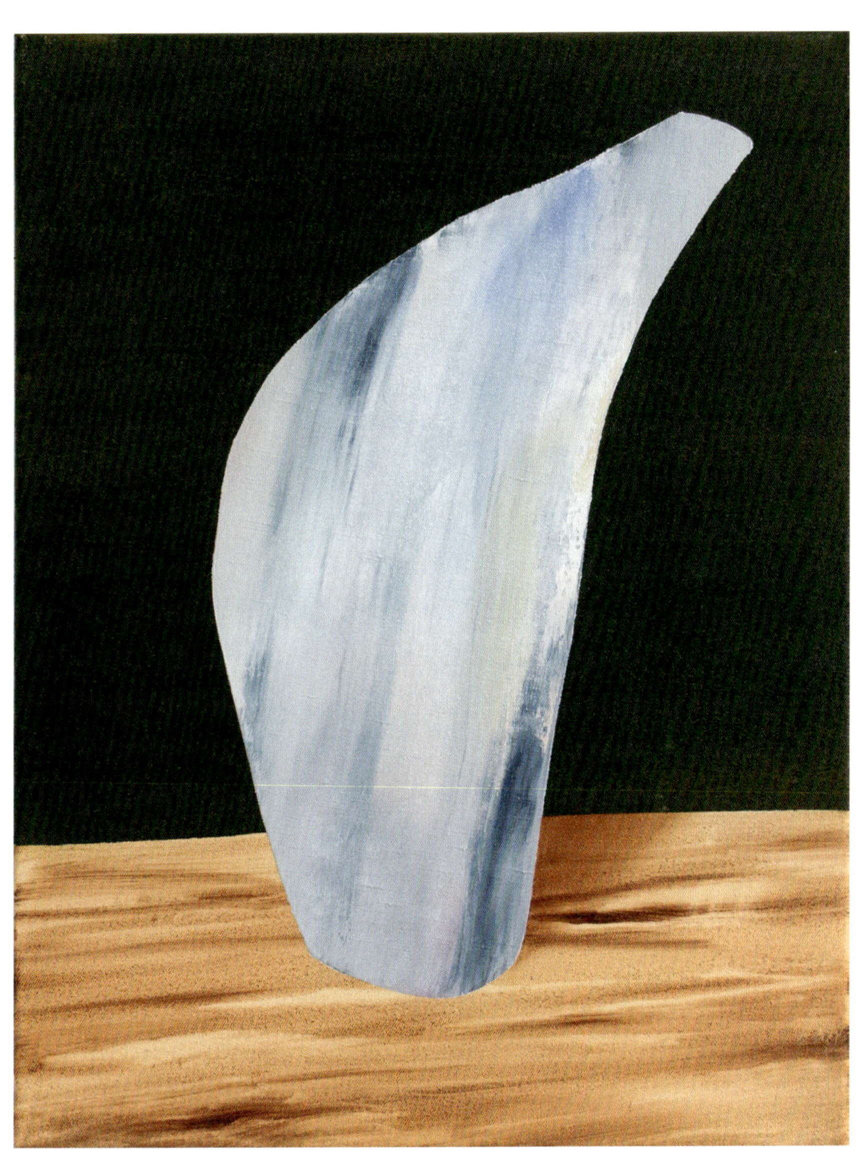

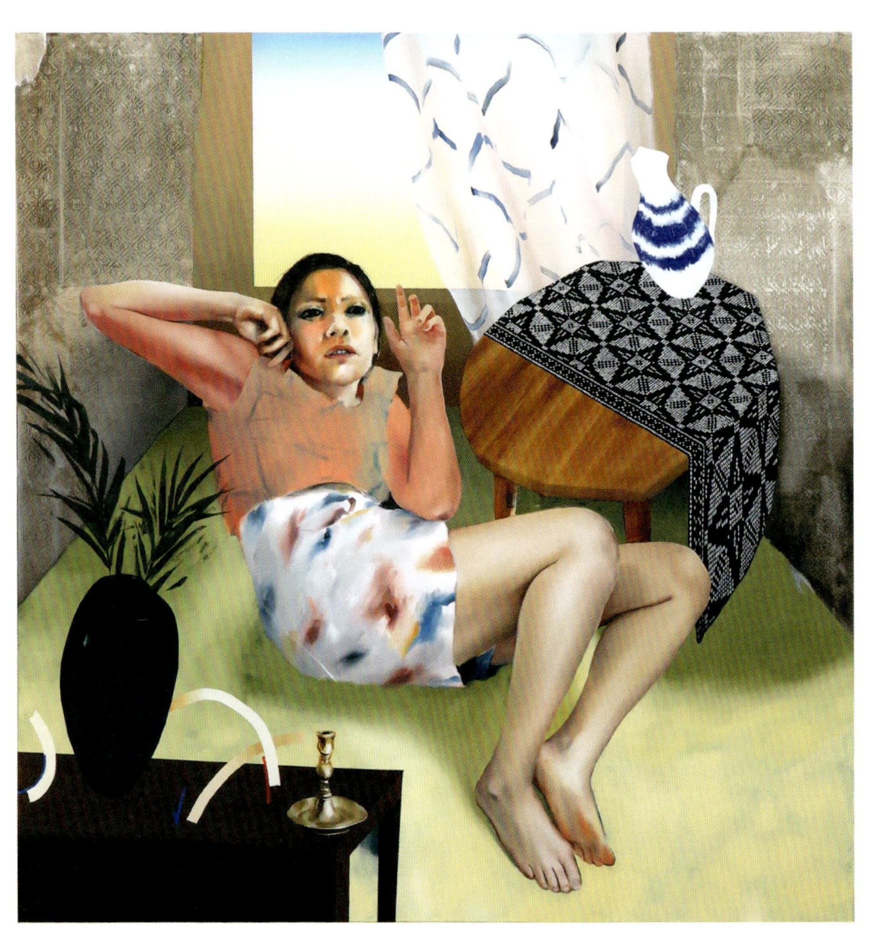

Couched

Öl auf Leinwand, 160 × 150 cm, 2018

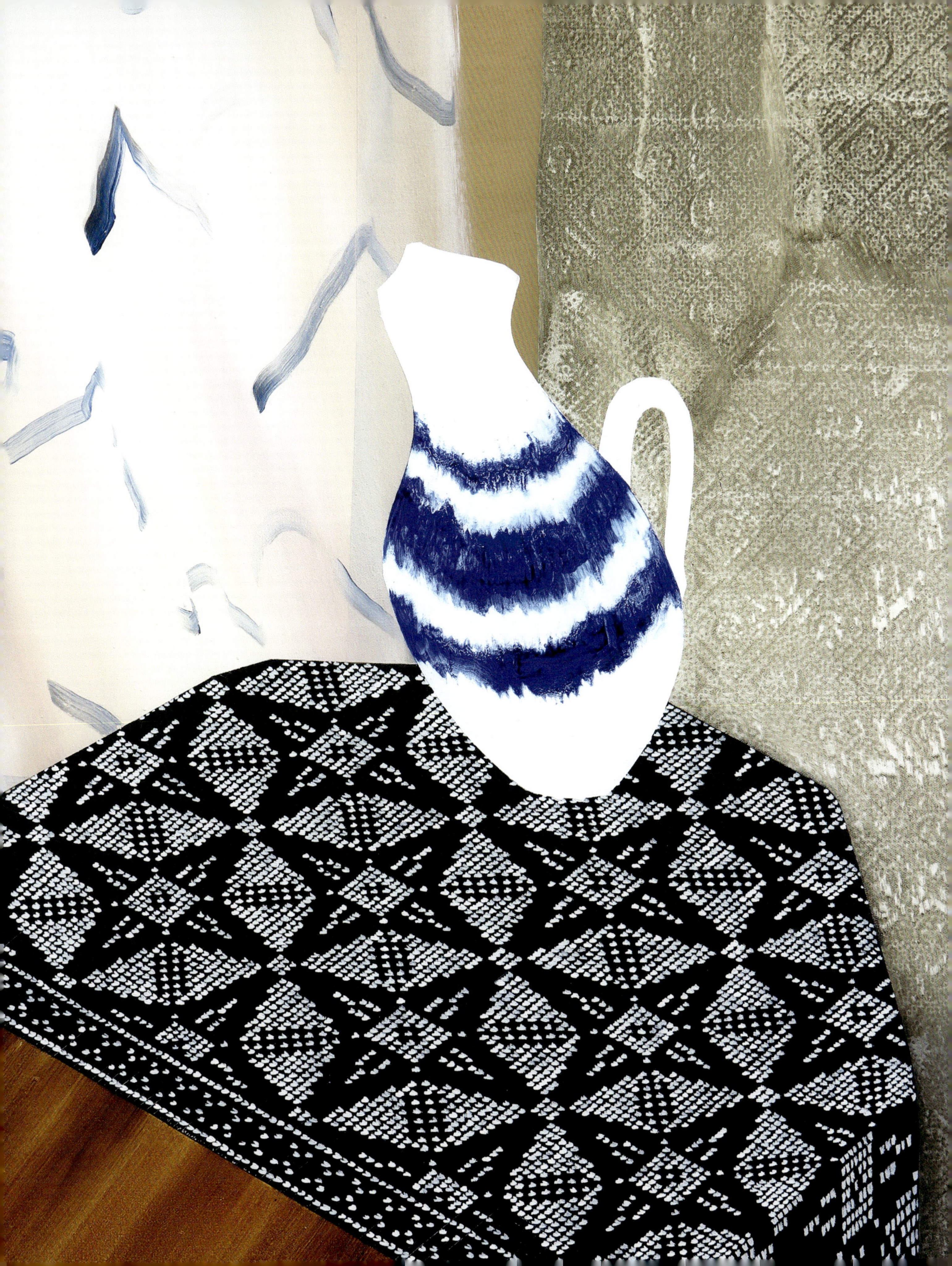

Speaking with Gesture

Öl auf Leinwand, 110 × 80 cm, 2019

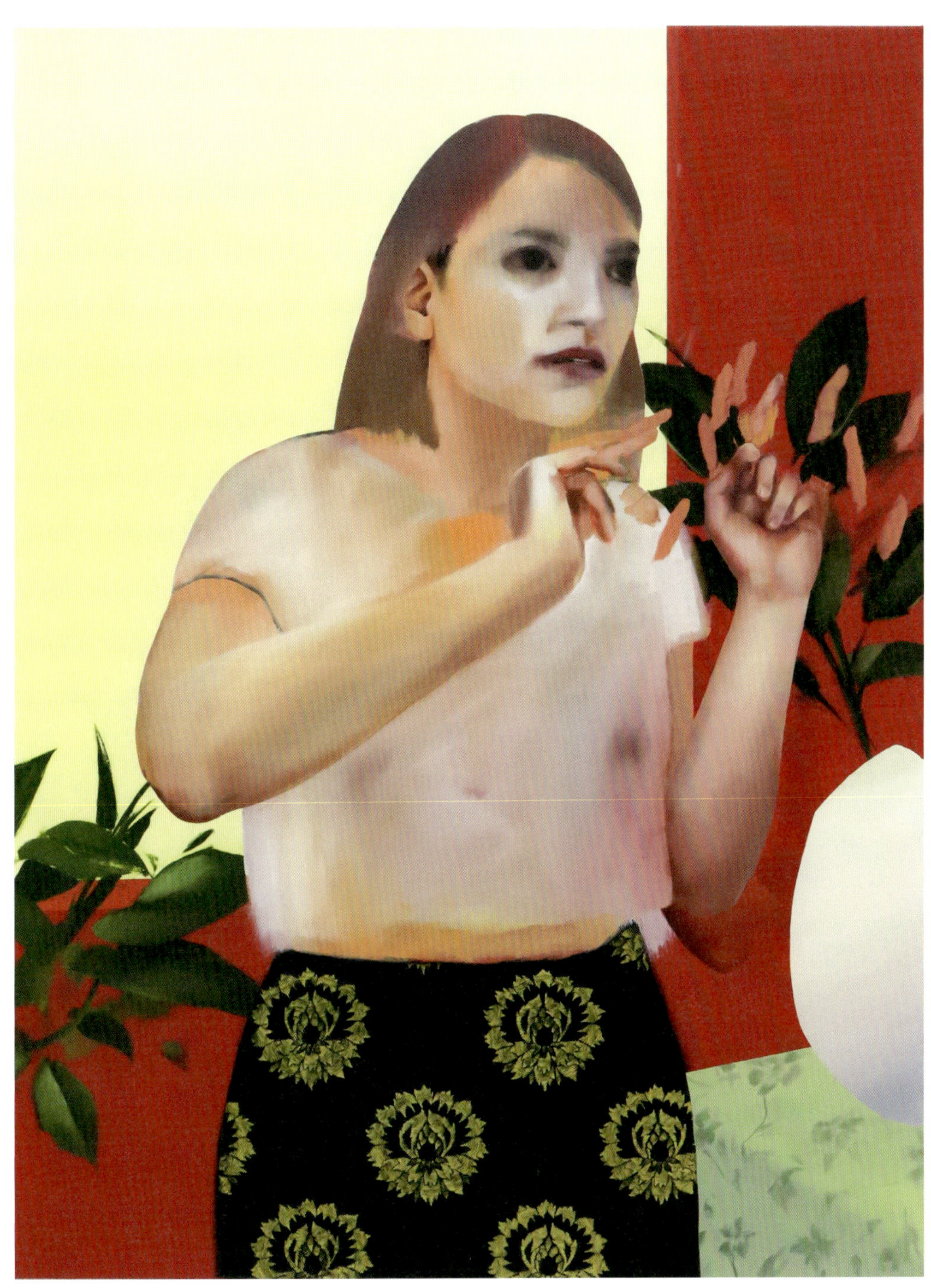

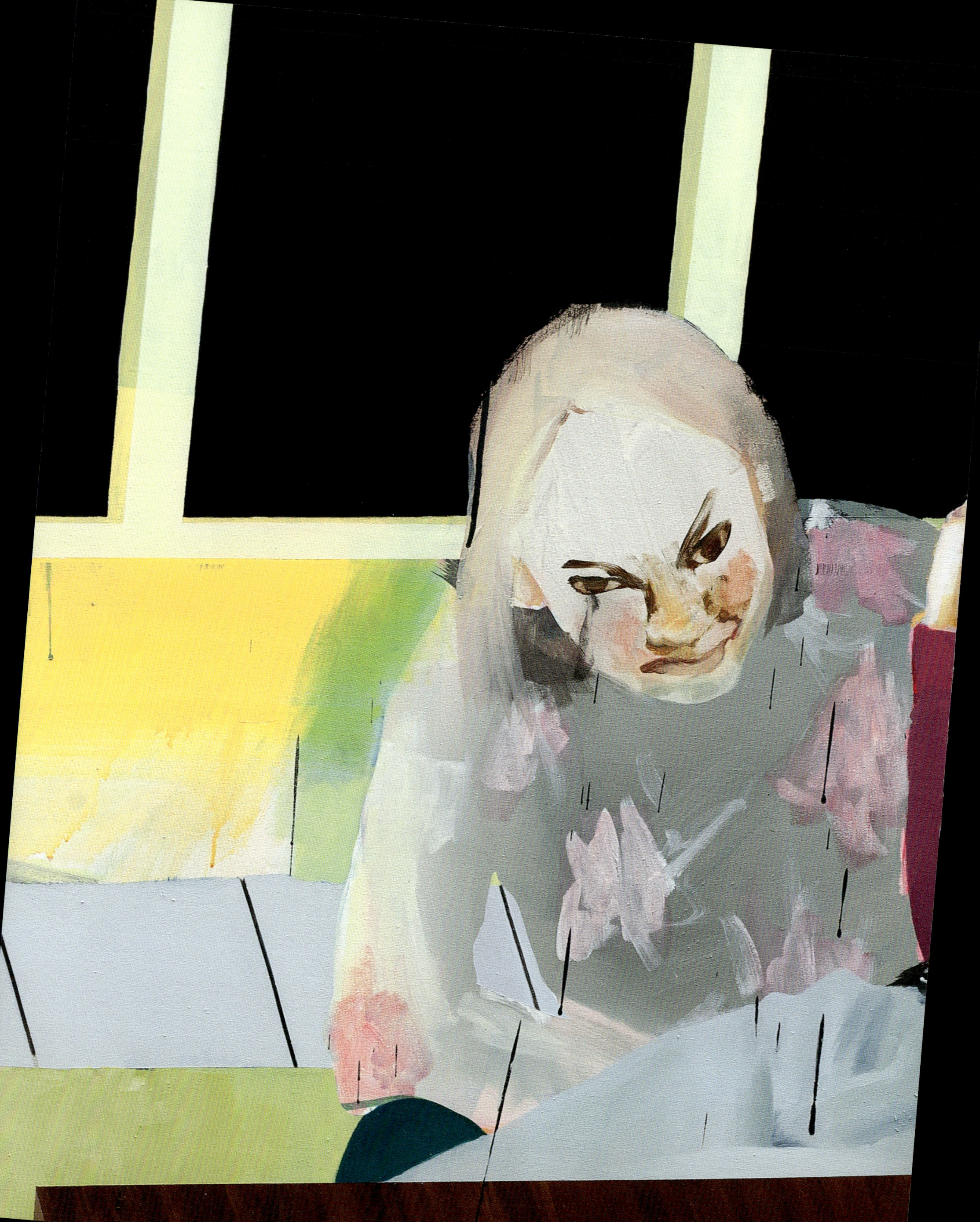

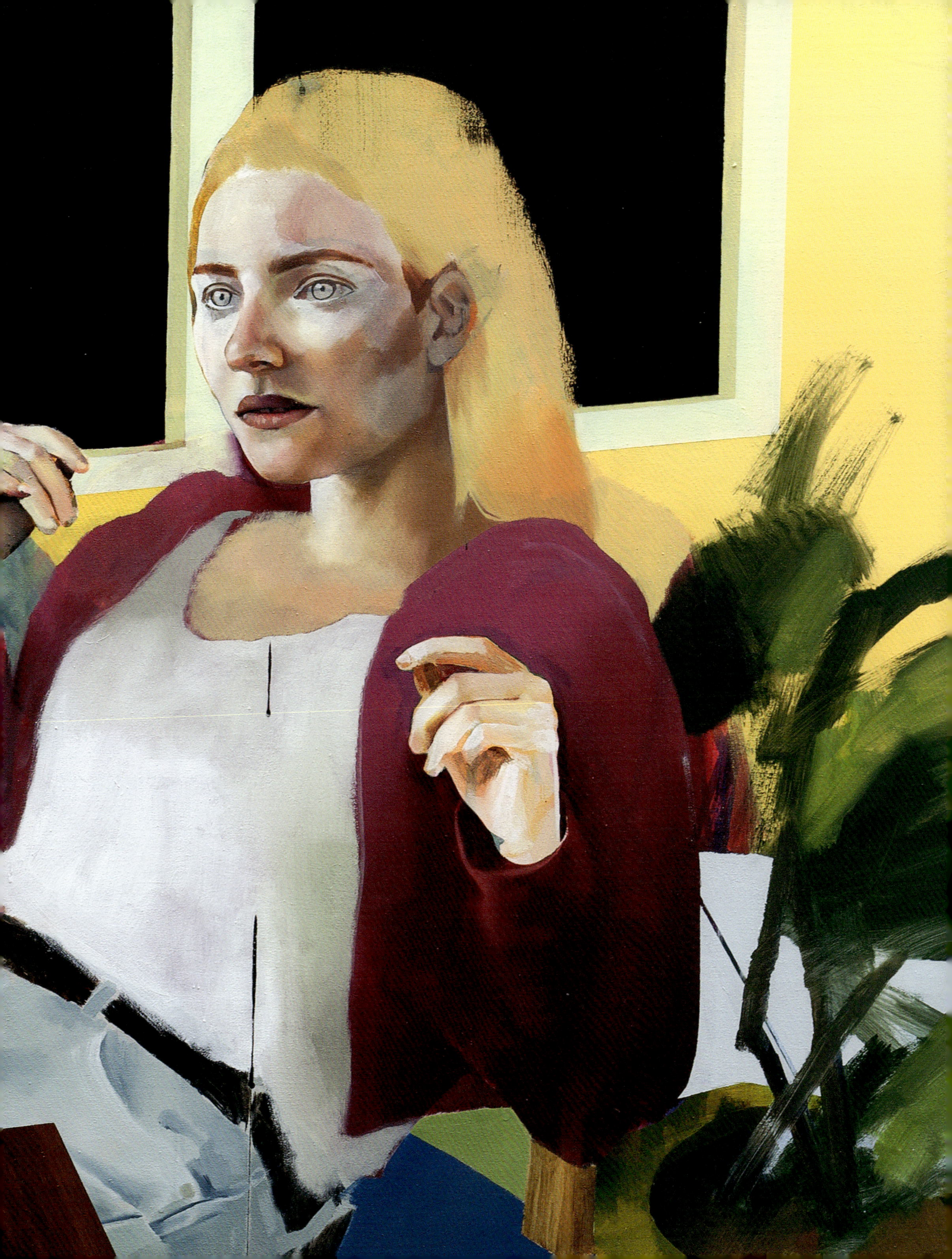

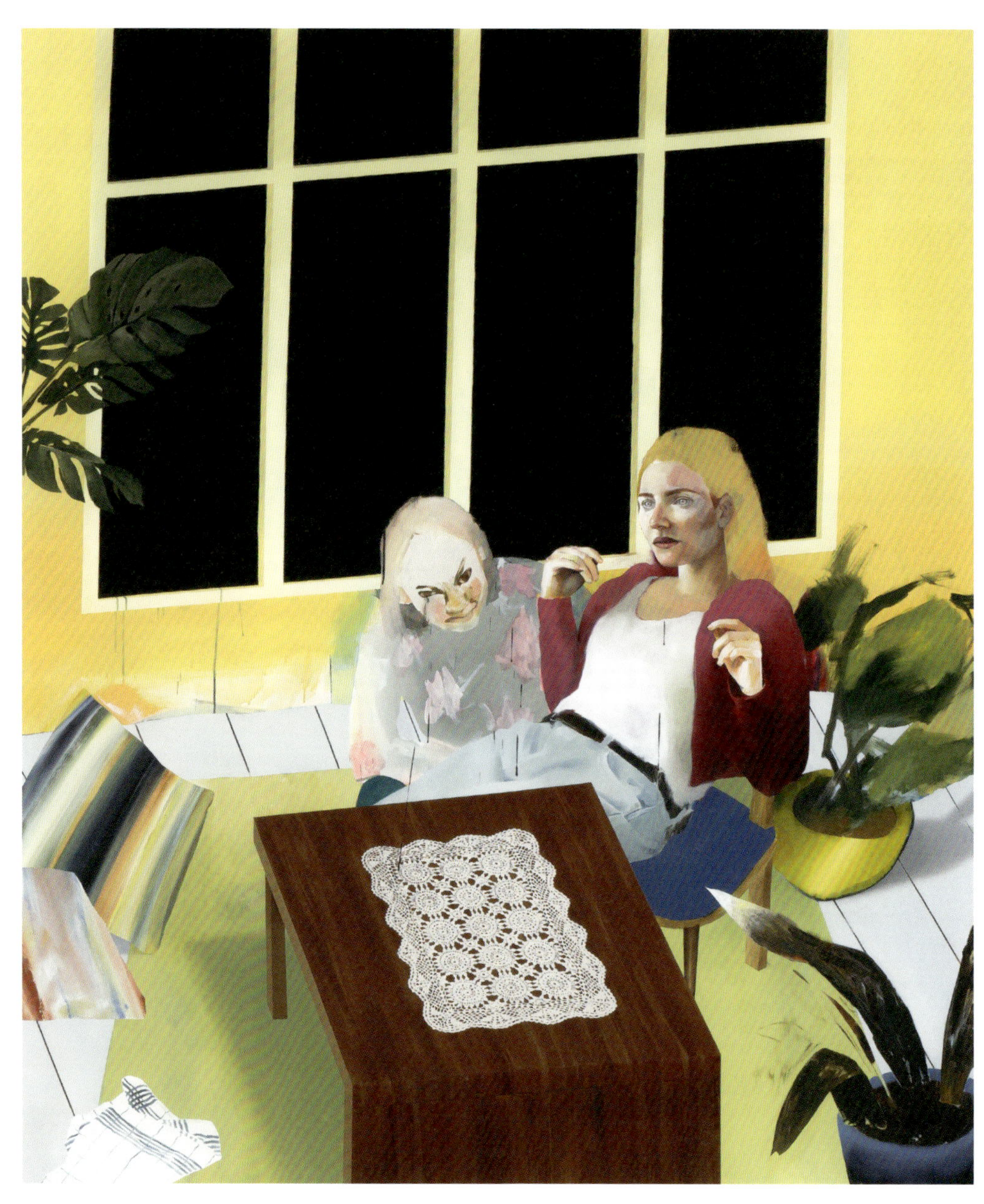

Nighttime

Öl und Acryl auf Leinwand, 220 × 180 cm, 2019

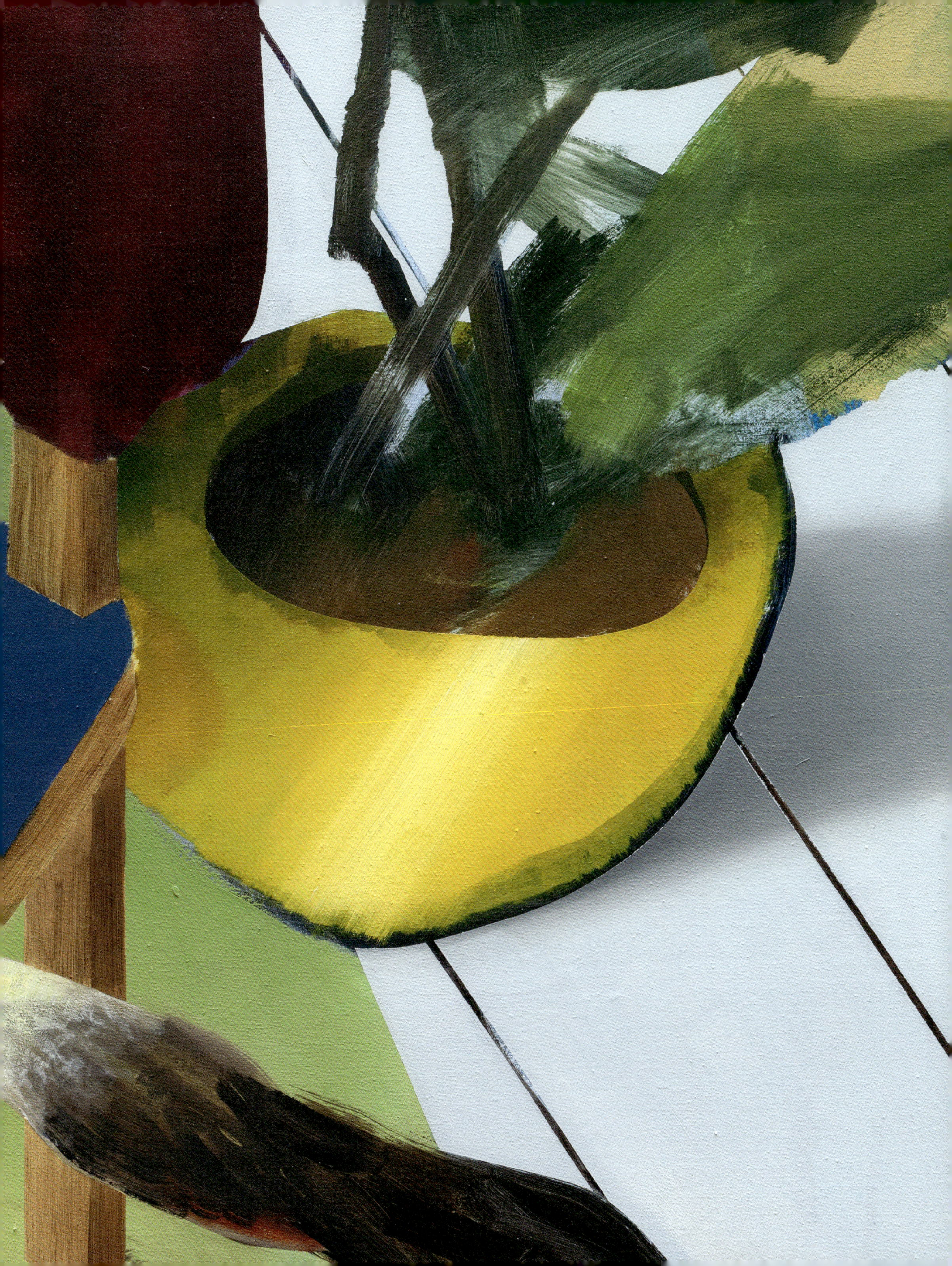

Unknowable Vase

Öl und Acryl auf Leinwand, 40×30 cm, 2019

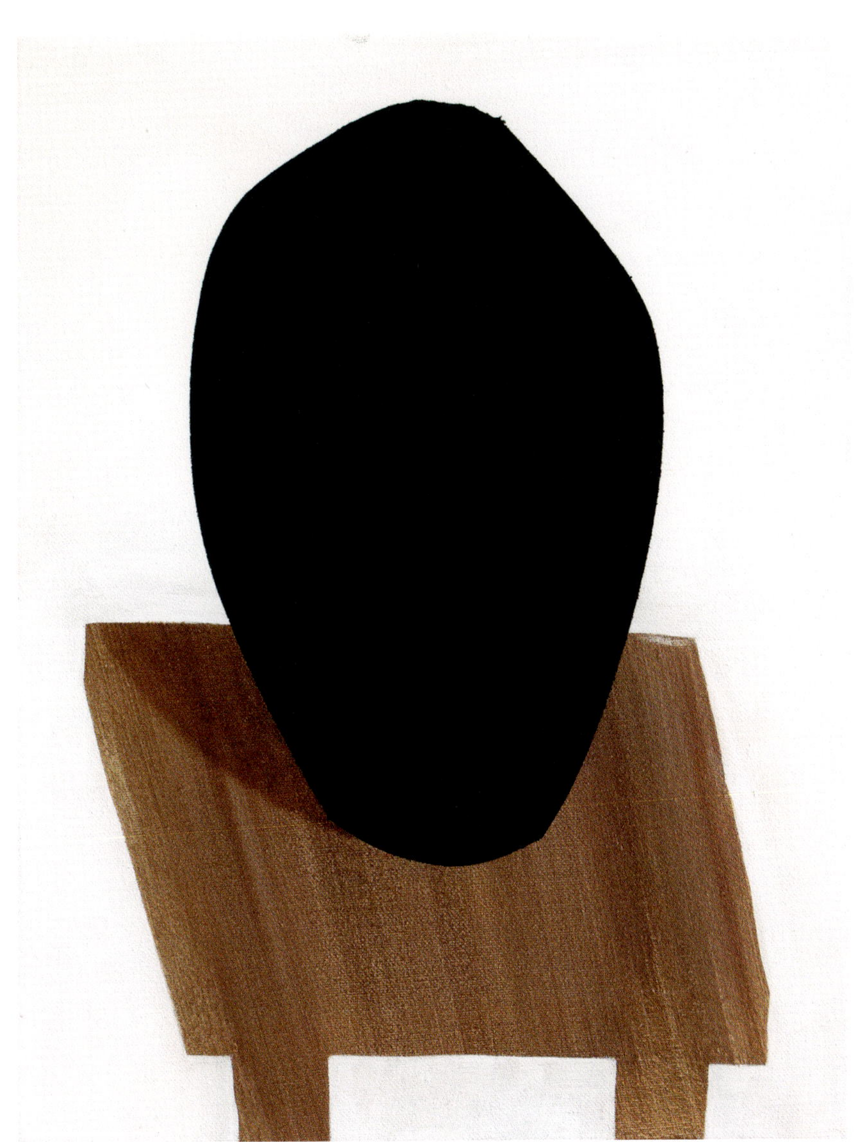

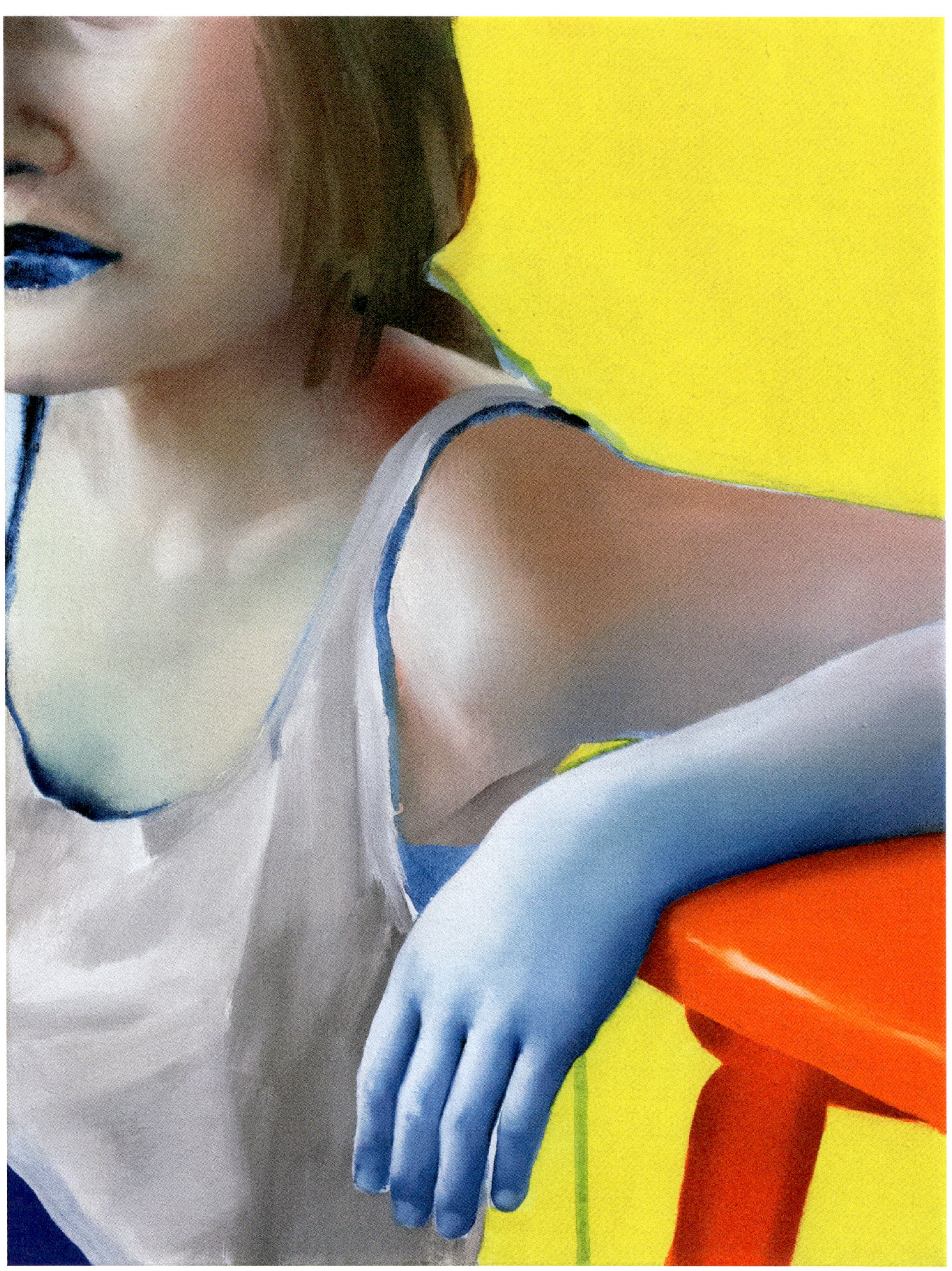

Blue Hand

Öl und Acryl auf Leinwand, 40 × 30 cm, 2020

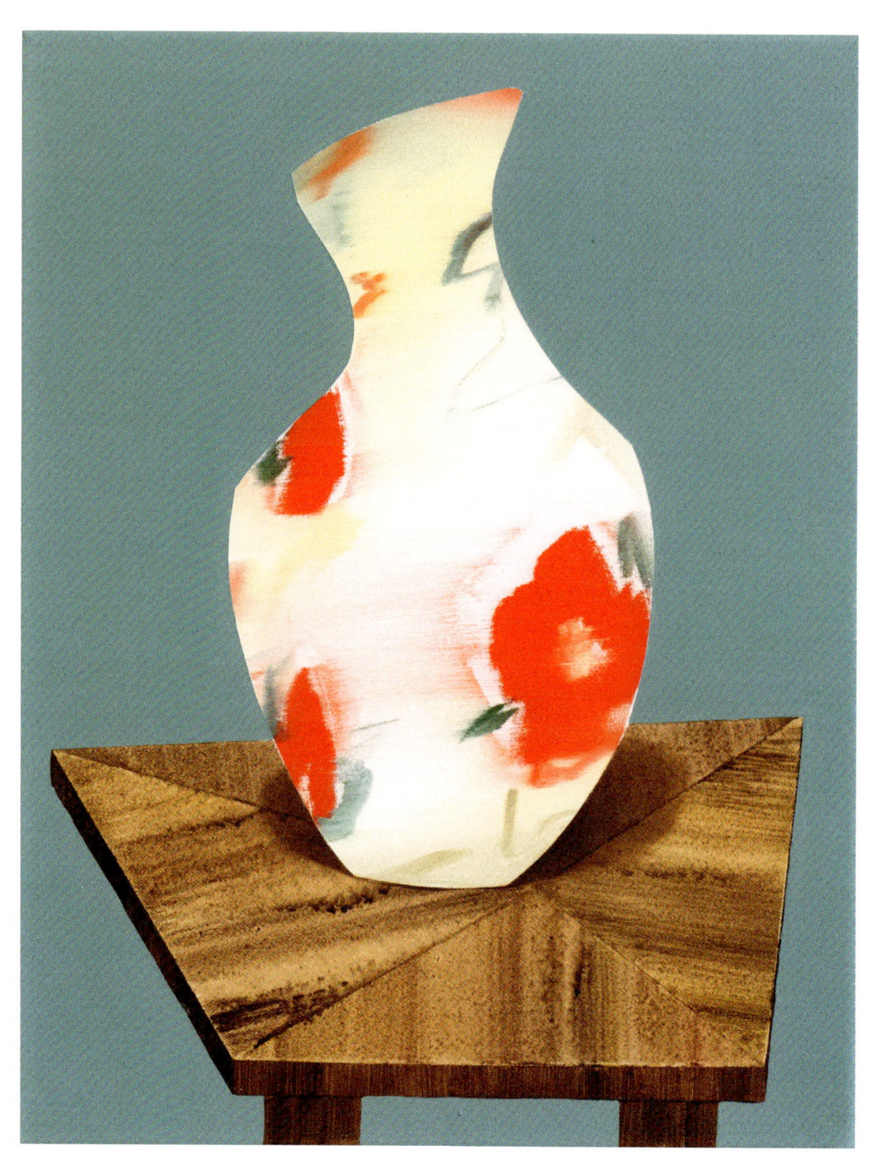

Floral Vase 1

Öl und Acryl auf Leinwand, 40×30 cm, 2019

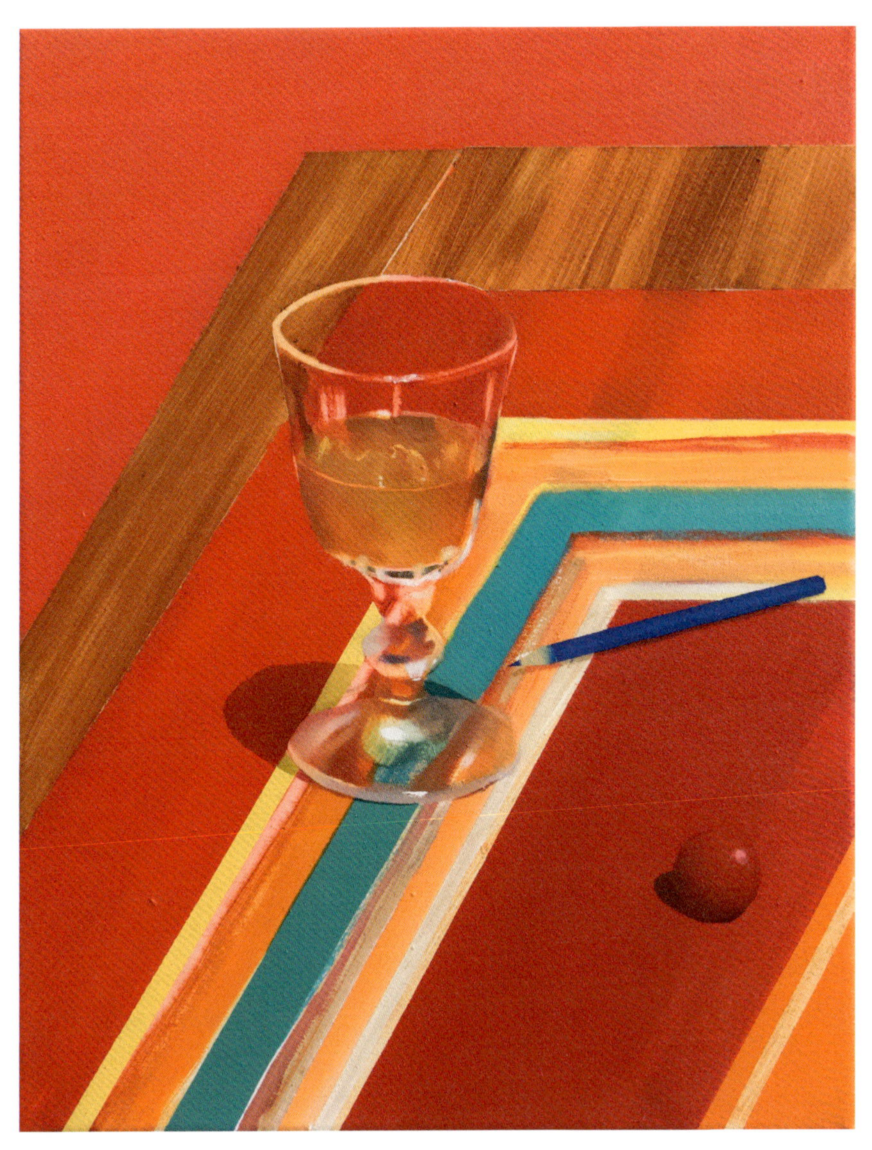

Red Still Life

Öl auf Leinwand, 40×30 cm, 2017

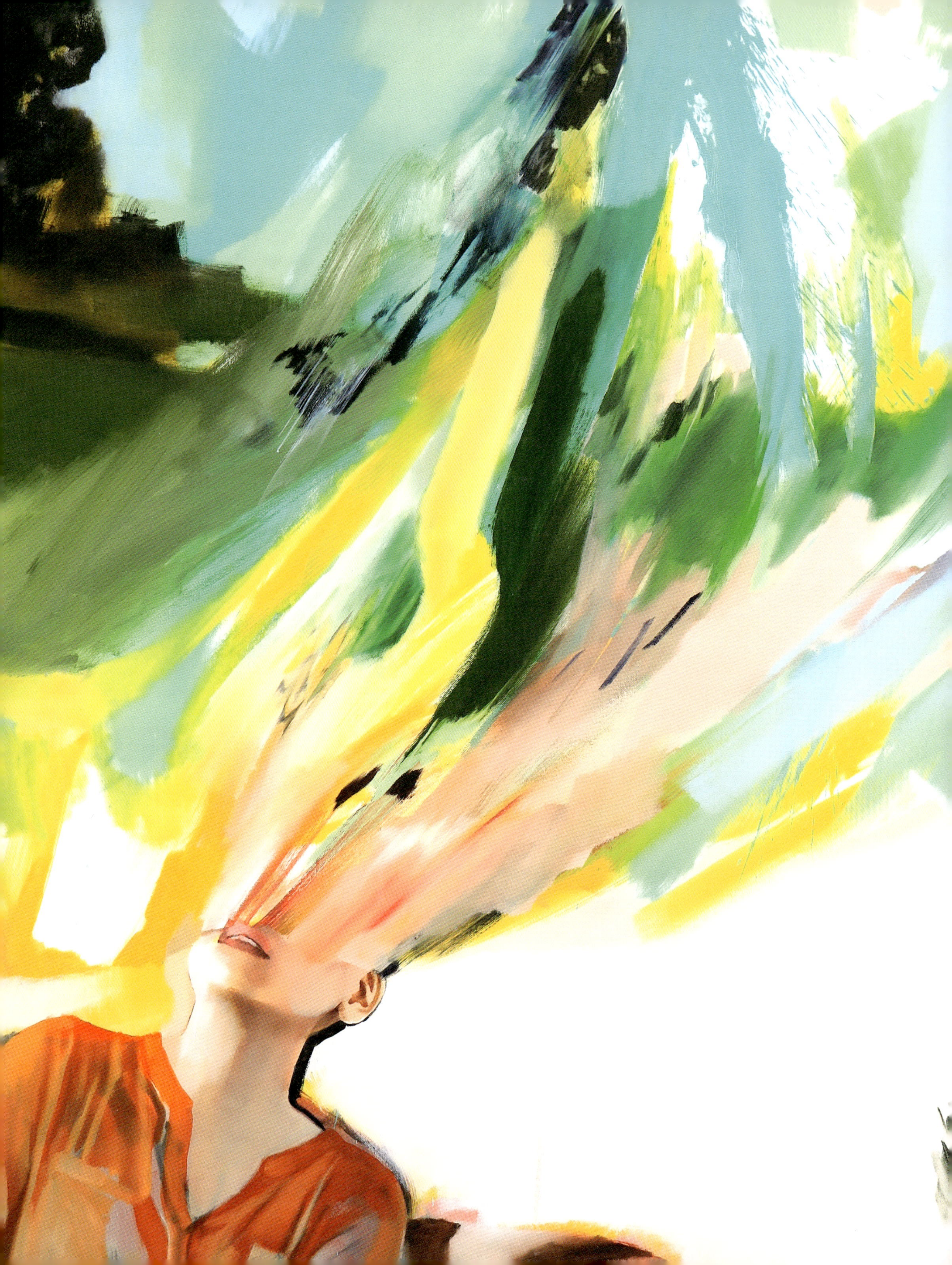

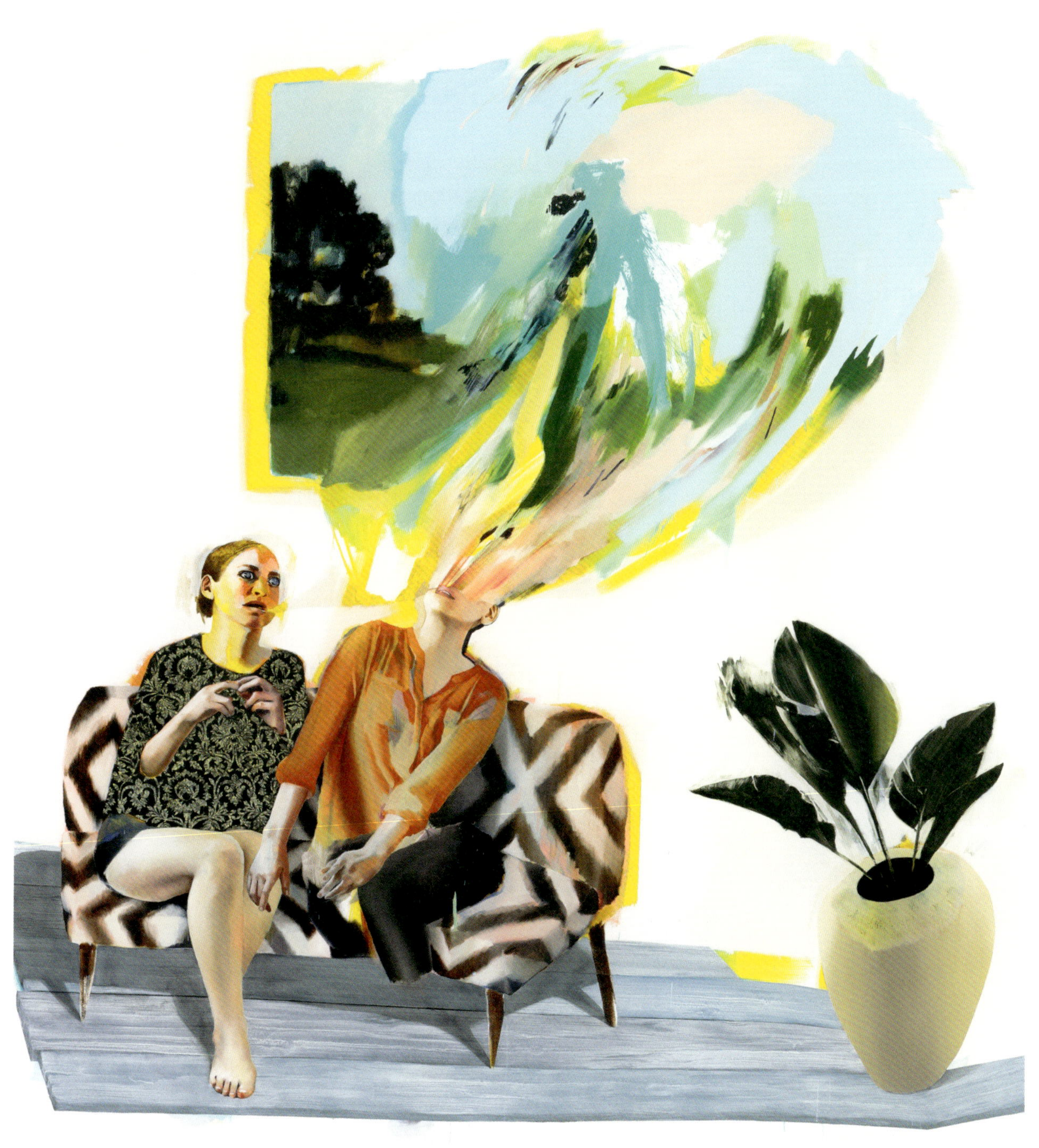

Speaking Persuasively

Öl auf Leinwand, 240 × 210 cm, 2018

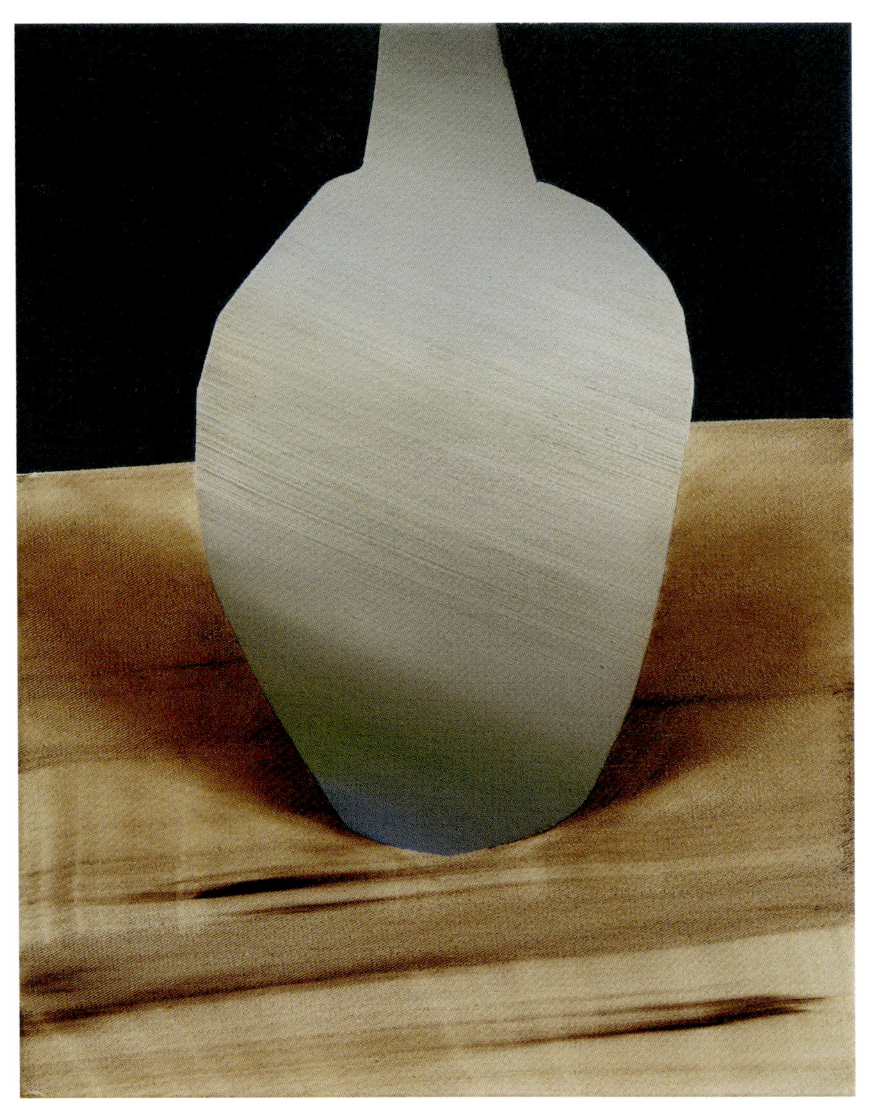

Double Shadow Vase

Öl auf Leinwand, 36×28 cm, 2017

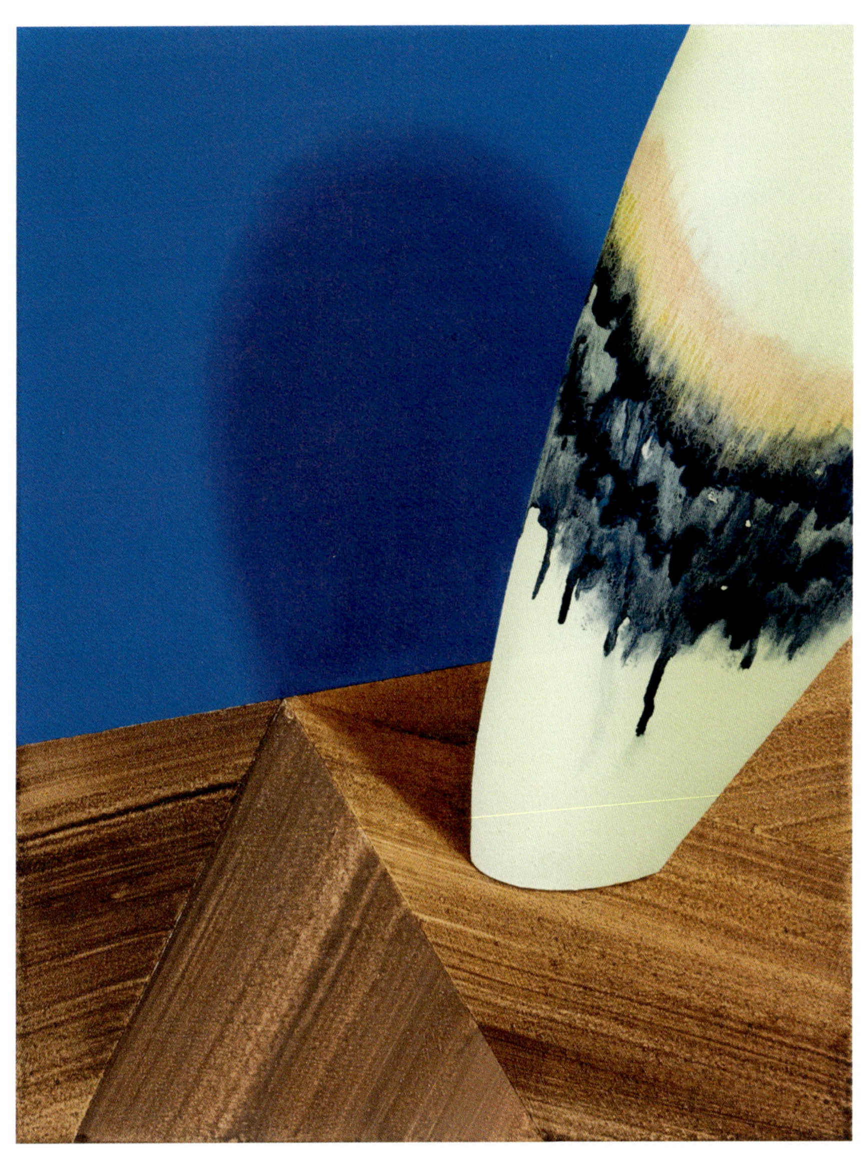

Dramatically Leaning Vase

Öl und Acryl auf Leinwand, 40 × 30 cm, 2019

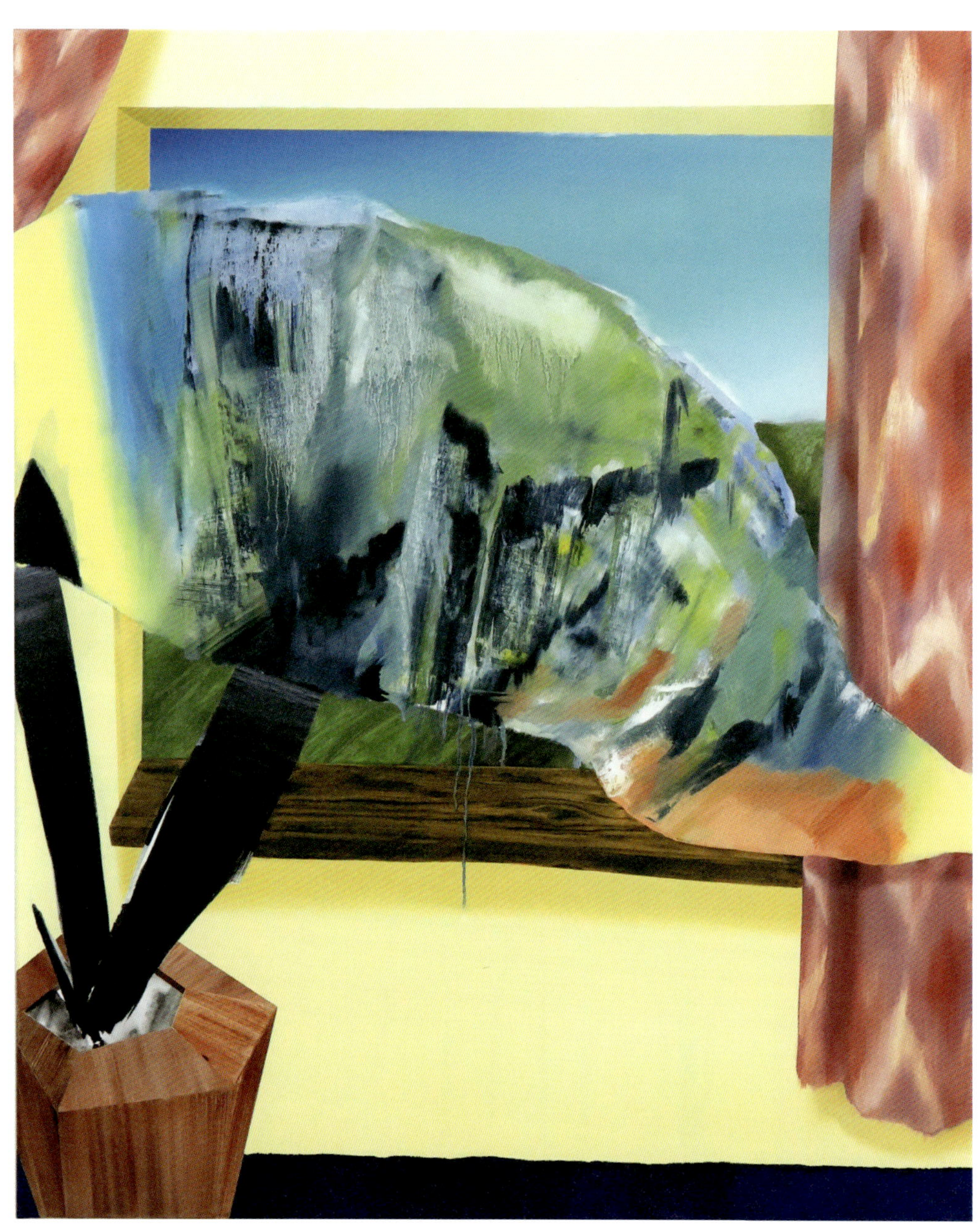

Talking Incomprehensibly About the Leaf

Öl und Acryl auf Leinwand, 100 × 80 cm, 2019

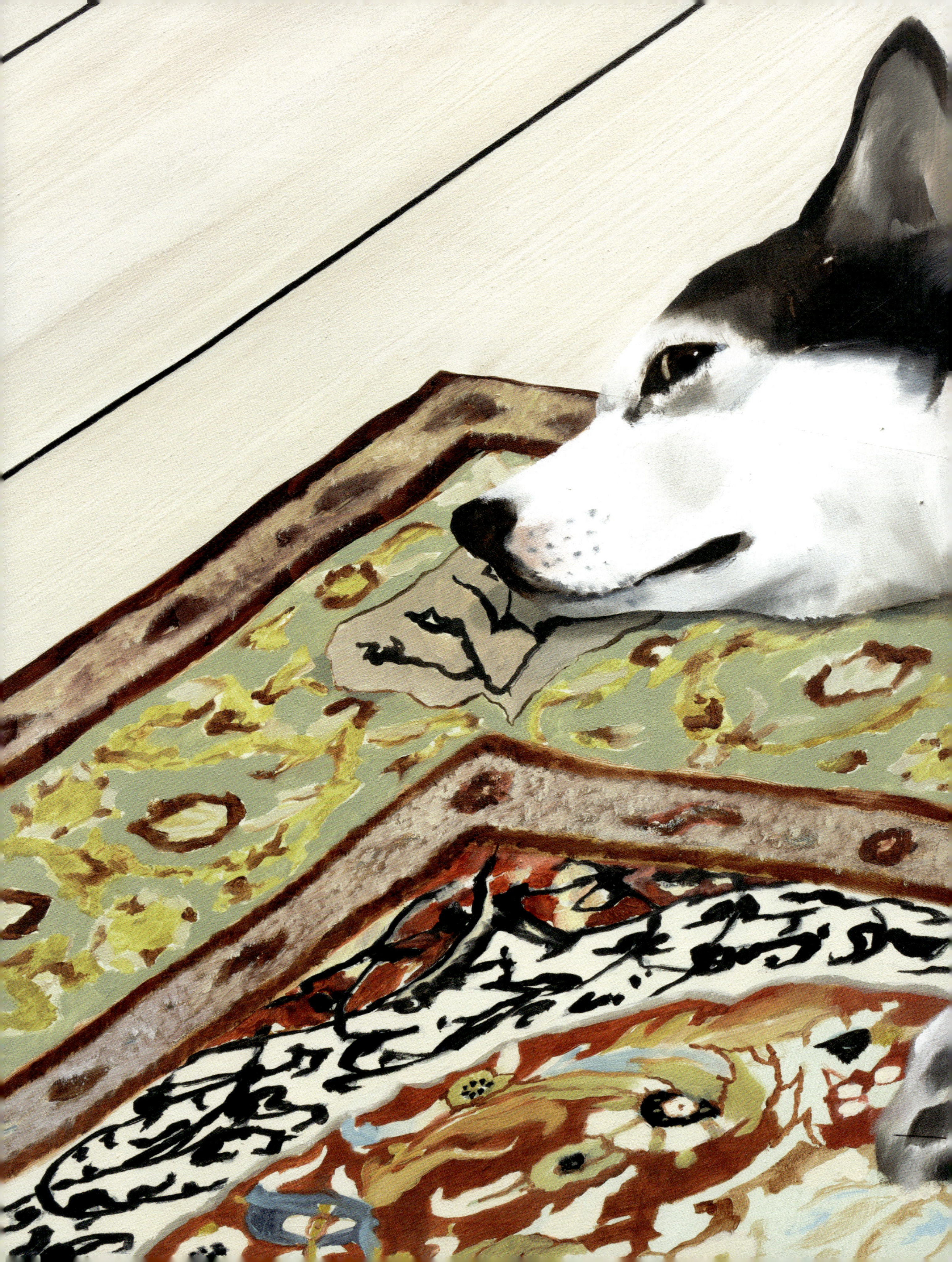

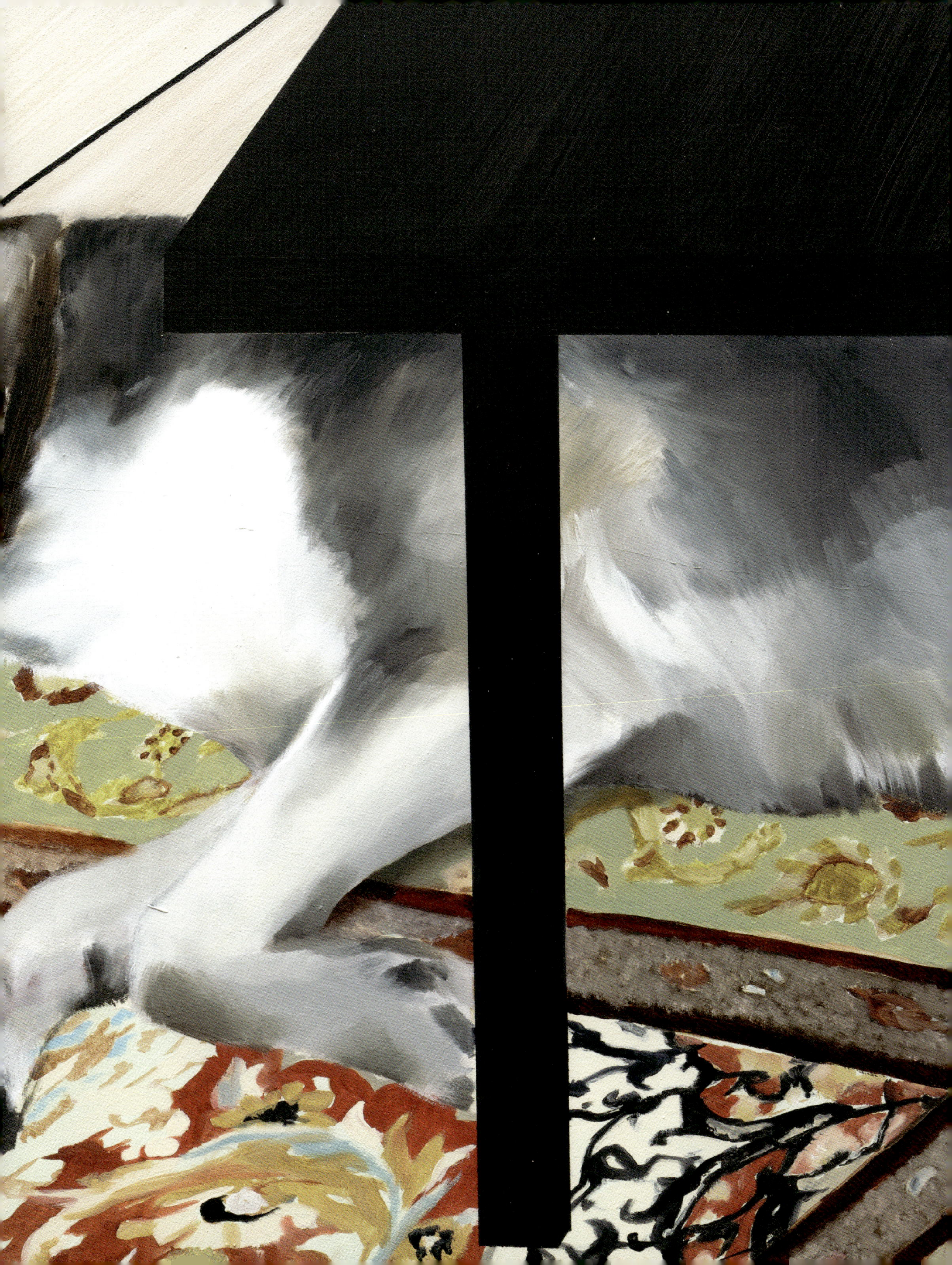

Thinking Around the Corner

Öl und Acryl auf Leinwand, 190×160 cm, 2020

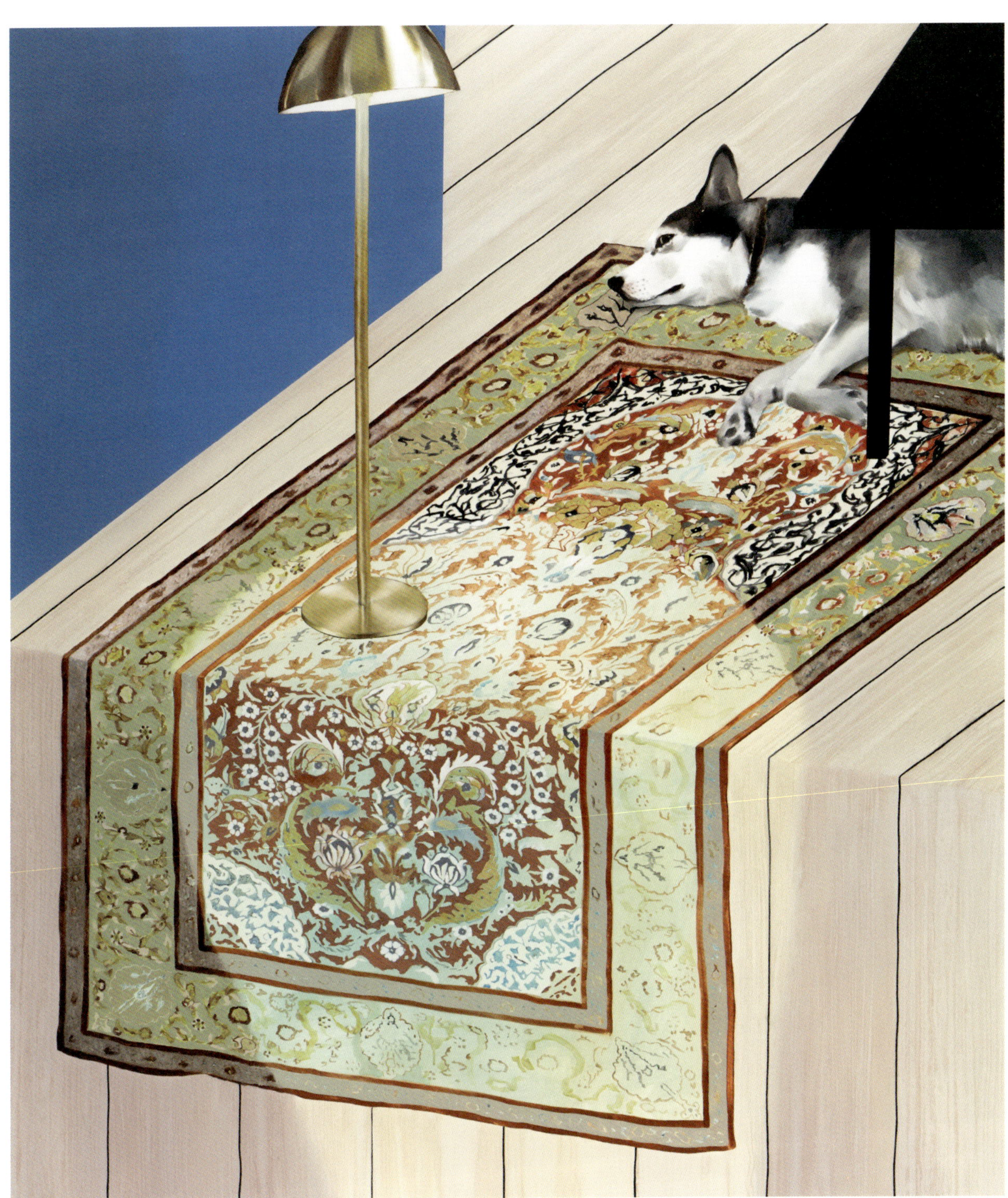

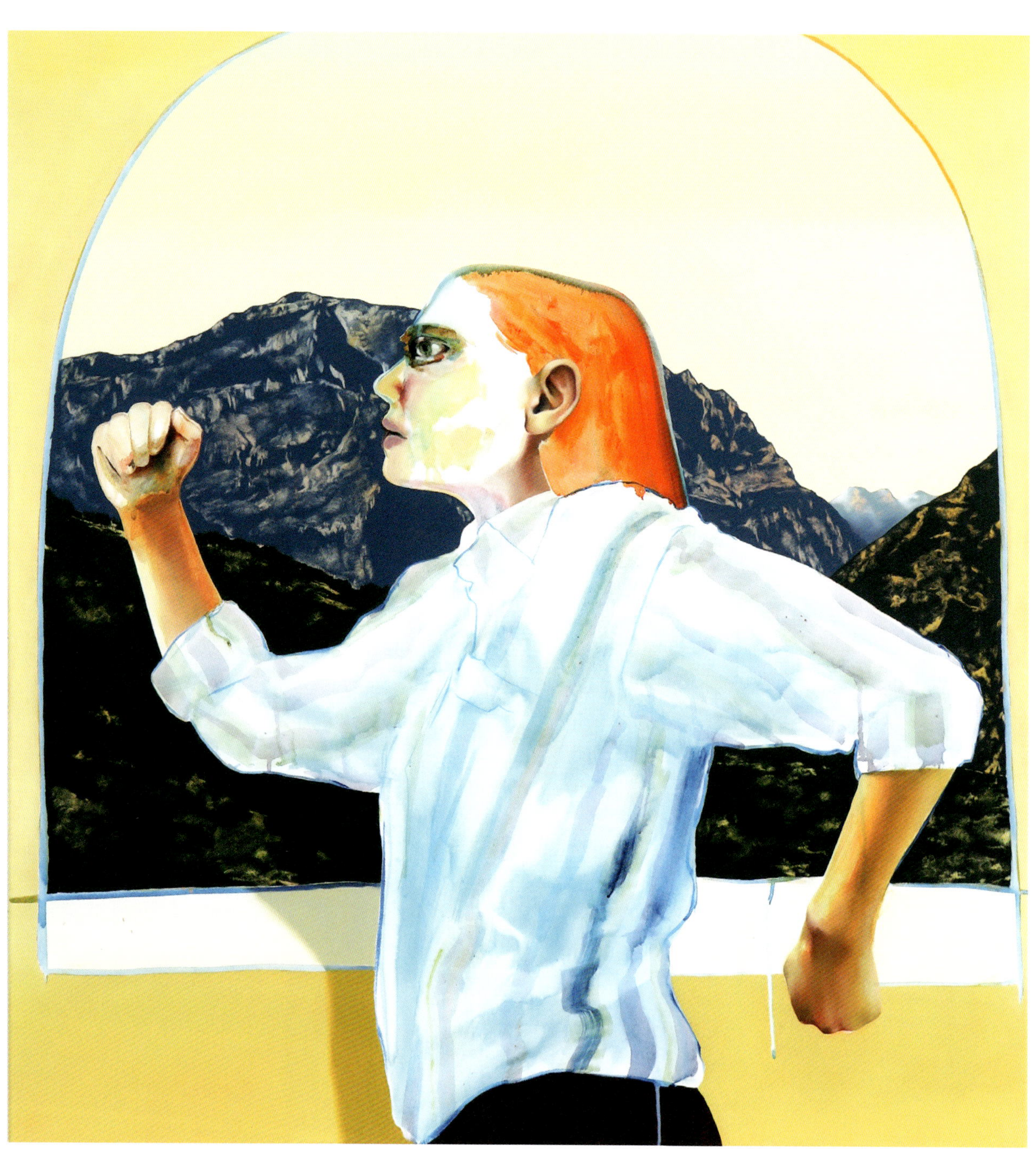

Running Heroically in Front of a Landscape

Öl und Acryl auf Leinwand, 110×100 cm, 2017

2016 into 2017

Öl und Collage auf Leinwand, 180 × 150 cm, 2017

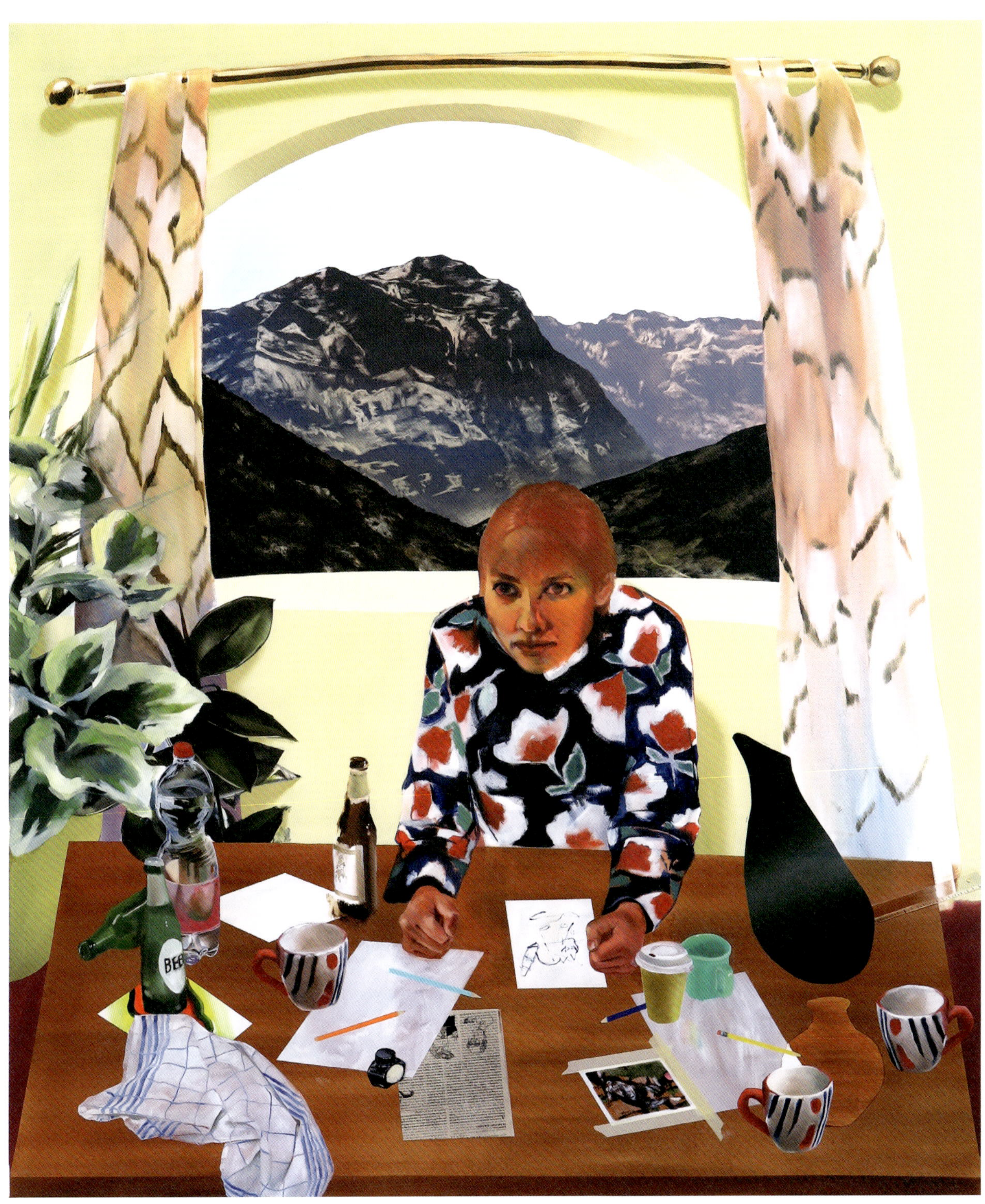

Ellen Akimoto

* 1988 in Westlake Village, Kalifornien (USA). Lebt und arbeitet in Leipzig.
** 1988 in Westlake Village, California. Lives and works in Leipzig, Germany.*

Ausbildung/*Education*

2014 – 2016 Meisterschülerin bei Prof. Annette Schröter an der Hochschule für Grafik und Buchkunst Leipzig (HGB)/*Postgraduate studies under Prof. Annette Schröter at the Academy of Fine Arts Leipzig*
2013 – 2014 Gaststudentin, Fachklasse Malerei/Grafik bei Prof. Annette Schröter an der HGB/*Guest student in the Painting/Printmaking class of Prof. Annette Schröter at the HGB*
2010 – 2011 Austauschjahr, Kunsthochschule Mainz, Fachklasse Prof. Anne Berning/*Exchange year at the Academy of Arts Mainz in the class of Prof. Anne Berning*
2006 – 2011 Bachelor of Fine Arts, California State University, Chico

Einzelausstellungen/*Solo Exhibitions*

2020 Creamy Feelings Curdle Galerie Rothamel, Frankfurt am Main
2019 Tilted Lens Galerie Oel-Früh, Hamburg
2017 PROTAGONISTS Galerie Rothamel, Frankfurt am Main
2013 Place Space Overdose Gallery, Chico, Kalifornien (USA)
2011 On, On, Pliant Signifier 1078 Gallery, Chico, Kalifornien (USA)
2010 Double Monologue BMU 3rd Floor Gallery, California State University, Chico, Kalifornien (USA)

Gruppenausstellungen*/*Group Exhibitions***

2020
SUPER! Kunsthalle Darmstadt
Minibar Galerie Oel-Früh, Hamburg
2019
Nous qui désirons sans fin Jeune Création, Paris
Painting Painting Painting Raum Vollreinigung, Berlin
2018
25. Leipziger Jahresausstellung: Silber Werkschauhalle/Halle 14, Leipzig
Congratulations! Kunstverein Speyer
SCOPE Galerie Rothamel, Erfurt
Nach dem Bild ist vor dem Bild – 75 Malerinnen aus Leipzig Kunstverein Freunde Aktueller Kunst, Zwickau
2017
Ausstellung zum Wettbewerb um die Hans-Purrmann-Preise 2017 Finalistin beim Großen Hans-Purrmann-Preis, Städtische Galerie Speyer
2016
Schön/Hide – Beautiful/Verstecken: Meisterklasse Annette Schröter Galerie Leuenroth, Frankfurt am Main/Galerie Elten & Elten, Zürich (CH)
Klassentreffen Kunsthalle der Sparkasse Leipzig
2015
Wunschlos Glücklich Kunstverein Duisburg
PR!NT La Cambre Galerie, Brüssel (BE)
Freistil Kunstverein Speyer
Screen Städtische Galerie Wolfsburg
2014
Stories 3 1078 Gallery, Chico, Kalifornien (USA)
2013
2012 Crocker-Kingsley Prizewinners The Crocker Art Museum, Sacramento, Kalifornien (USA)
2012
Stories 1 1078 Gallery, Chico, Kalifornien (USA)

Preise Und Stipendien*/
*Awards And Scholarships***

2019 Elizabeth Greenshields Foundation Grant
2018 Anerkennung der Jury für den Preis der 25. Leipziger Jahresausstellung 2018
2018 Arbeitsstipendium von der Kulturstiftung des Freistaates Sachsen
2015 DAAD Study Scholarship for Foreign Graduates. Stipendium
2012 Merit Award (Auszeichnung), The Crocker-Kingsley Competition, Blue Line Gallery
2011 Preis des Präsidenten, Johannes Gutenberg Universität, Mainz

*(Auswahl)/***(Selection)*

Impressum

Diese Publikation erscheint anlässlich der Ausstellung: *This publication is released to accompany the exhibition:*

Ellen Akimoto, Creamy Feelings Curdle, Galerie Rothamel

Herausgeber / *Editor:*
GALERIE ROTHAMEL
www.rothamel.de
galerie@rothamel.de
Kleine Arche 1A, 99084 Erfurt, Germany
Fahrgasse 17, 60311 Frankfurt am Main, Germany
+49 361 562 33 96
+49 177 599 84 45

Text:
Wolfgang Ullrich

Gestaltung / *Design*:
Jan Motyka

Übersetzung / *Translation*:
Michael Reid

Fotos / *Photos*:
Ellen Akimoto, Gustav Franz, Thomas John

Projektmanagement / *Project Management*,
Kerber Verlag: Lydia Fuchs

Herstellung / *Production*,
Kerber Verlag: Jens Bartneck

Gesamtherstellung / *Printed and published by*:
Kerber Verlag, Bielefeld
Windelsbleicher Str. 166–170
33659 Bielefeld, Germany
Tel. +49 (0) 5 21/9 50 08-10
Fax +49 (0) 5 21/9 50 08-88
info@kerberverlag.com
kerberverlag.com

KERBER Publikationen werden weltweit vertrieben / *Kerber publications are distributed worldwide:*

ACC Art Books
Sandy Lane
Old Martlesham
Woodbridge, IP12 4SD, UK
+44 1394 38 99 50
+44 1394 38 99 99 (F)
accartbooks.com

Artbook | D.A.P.
75 Broad Street, Suite 630
New York, NY 10004, USA
+1 212 627 19 99
+1 212 627 94 84 (F)
artbook.com

AVA Verlagsauslieferung Scheidegger
Obere Bahnhofstr. 10A
8910 Affoltern am Albis
Switzerland
+41 44 762 42 41
+41 44 762 42 49 (F)
avainfo@ava.ch

KNV Zeitfracht
Verlagsauslieferung
kerber-verlag@knv-zeitfracht.de

Die Deutsche Nationalbibliothek verzeichnet diese Publikation in der Deutschen Nationalbibliografie: dnb.de. / *The Deutsche Nationalbibliothek lists this publication in the Deutsche Nationalbibliografie: dnb.de.*

ISBN 978-3-7356-0714-0

www.kerberverlag.com

Printed in Germany

Dieses Buch wurde durch eine Förderung des Kulturamts Leipzig ermöglicht. / *This book was sponsored in part by the Cultural Office of the city of Leipzig.*

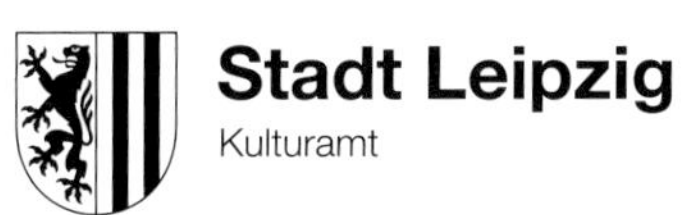

Die Entstehung der in diesem Buch präsentierten Werke wurde durch Stipendien der Elizabeth Greenshields Stiftung und der Kulturstiftung des Freistaates Sachsen ermöglicht. / *The creation of the works presented in this book was facilitated by grants from the Elizabeth Greenshields Foundation and the Cultural Foundation of the Free State of Saxony.*

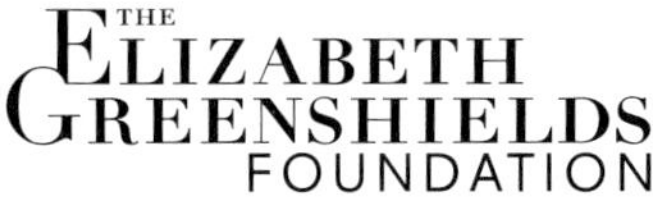

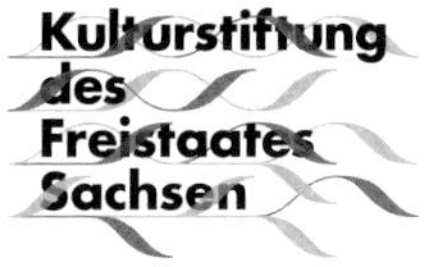

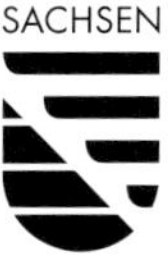

Gefördert durch die Kulturstiftung des Freistaates Sachsen. Diese Maßnahme wird mitfinanziert durch Steuermittel auf der Grundlage des vom Sächsischen Landtag beschlossenen Haushaltes.

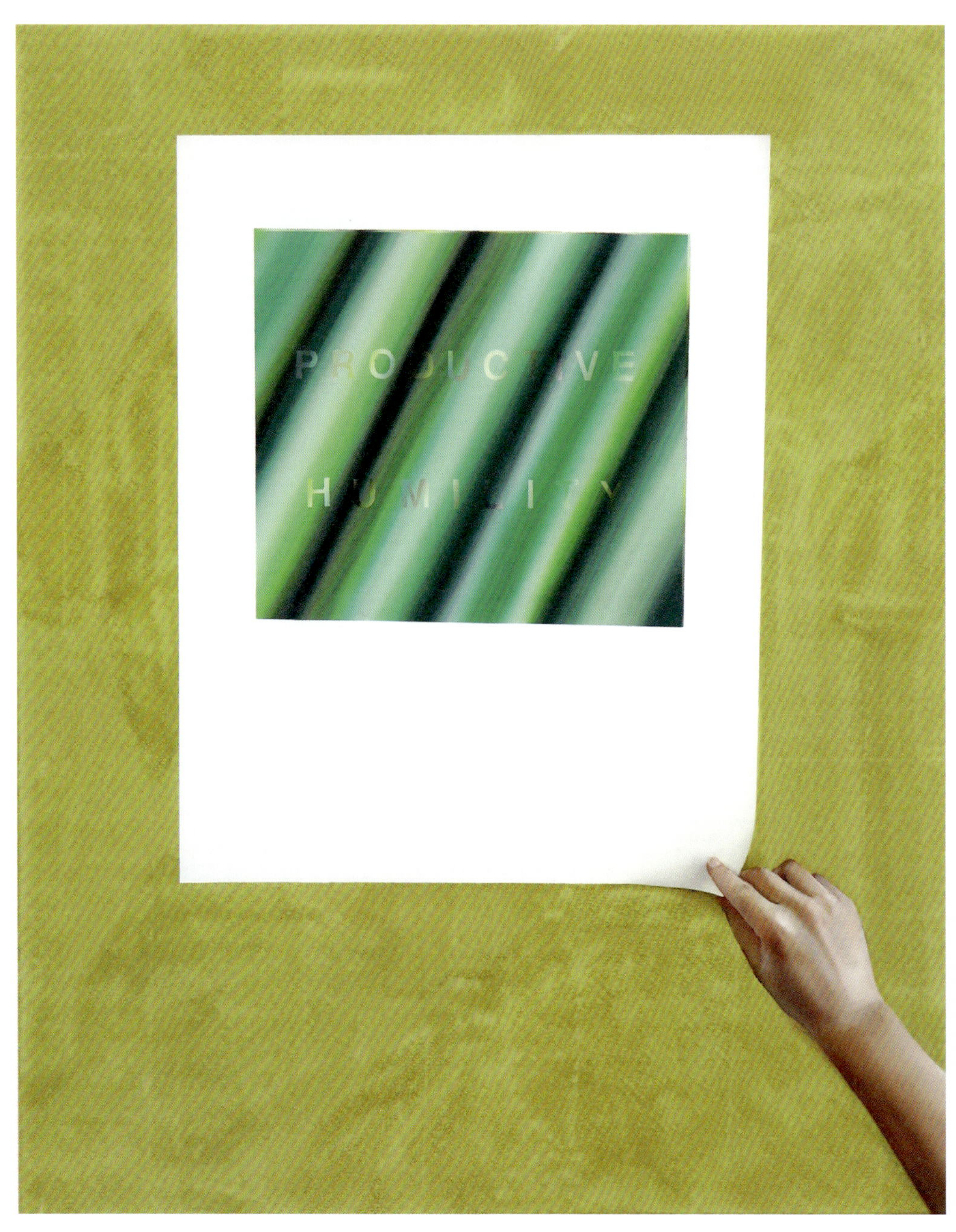

Productive Humility

Öl auf Leinwand, 90×70 cm, 2018